RECOVERY

A Handbook of Twelve-Step
Key Terms and Phrases

Central Recovery Press would like to thank all
the individuals whose thoughtful input and suggestions
have made this a much better handbook.

CENTRAL RECOVERY PRESS

LAS VEGAS, NEVADA

CENTRAL RECOVERY PRESS

Central Recovery Press (CRP) is committed to publishing exceptional material addressing addiction treatment and recovery, including original and quality books, audio/visual communications, and web-based new media. Through a diverse selection of titles, it seeks to impact the behavioral healthcare field with a broad range of unique resources for professionals, recovering individuals, and their families. For more information, visit www.centralrecoverypress.com.

CRP donates a portion of its proceeds to Foundation for Recovery, a nonprofit organization local and national in scope. Its purpose is to promote recovery from addiction through a variety of forums, such as direct services, research and development, education, study of recovery alternatives, public awareness, and advocacy.

Central Recovery Press, Las Vegas, NV 89129
© 2009 by Central Recovery Press, Las Vegas, NV

ISBN-13: 978-0-9799869-3-2

ISBN-10: 0-9799869-3-1

15 14 13 12 11 10 09   1 2 3 4 5

Publisher: Central Recovery Press
              3371 N Buffalo Drive
              Las Vegas, NV 89129

Cover design and interior by Sara Streifel, Think Creative Design

Contents

Introduction

Twelve-step programs have a language of their own. While there are numerous adaptations of the original Twelve Steps, much of the language is the same across all these programs. This handbook is designed to give those new to twelve-step recovery and friends and family members of persons in recovery, as well as those who have been in the program for a while, a starting point from which they will hopefully develop or expand their own understanding of many of the terms used in meetings and program literature. The words and concepts in this handbook are specific to the Twelve Steps and many recovery programs. We realize that some of these words and concepts have more general meanings as well.

We hope that providing a simple and easy-to-understand reference guide will help you make sense of "twelve-step language" and help to translate the experience of recovery.

It also may be of help to friends and family who are often just as baffled by the newfound recovery life of their loved one as they were by that person's active addiction. Their loved one had been on the brink of death, and now, in a relatively short period of time, he or she is zealously attending meetings every day and becoming completely engrossed in a healthy and welcome, but equally consuming (and perhaps confusing) lifestyle, complete with a new vocabulary and new ways of expressing him- or herself. A simple handbook is not going to solve this problem; sincere and ongoing communication, whatever the words used, will help far more, but again, this is a starting point.

People with some time in the program know better than anyone that understanding and experience changes constantly in recovery. In fact, it is said "the only constant is change." This handbook can be helpful to those with long-term recovery as they work with newer members, and also can help give the more experienced member a deeper, broader understanding of many of the definitions with which they are familiar.

This book was written with the input and contributions of members of twelve-step recovery programs. It is not meant to be a definitive work on the subject nor is it written by "professionals" in recovery or the treatment community.

This first edition is just that—the first. It will evolve over time just as the members of twelve-step programs do. As more information and feedback is gathered from readers, the more comprehensive the definitions will become. We realize that some words and concepts are missing, and promise that as work on the second edition begins, those words will be added.

Send Us What We Missed

We know there are many words and concepts we missed from the scores of twelve-step fellowships that are around today. We invite you to send us any words, concepts, slogans, or any other input that you may use in your fellowship, but wasn't included in this handbook. It is our goal to make this as comprehensive as possible, as well as a book that is accessible to members of twelve-step fellowships and the general public. This is truly a work-in-progress.

How to Submit Your Input

MAIL

Central Recovery Press
Recovery A–Z Submissions
3371 North Buffalo Drive
Las Vegas, NV 89129

EMAIL

CentralRecoveryPress@centralrecovery.com

FAX

(702) 396-3501

FOR OTHER INFORMATION

Visit CentralRecoveryPress.com.

ABSTINENCE and/or ABSTINENT

Self-denial, self-restraint, self-disciplined. Not using any mind- or mood-altering chemicals or drugs, including alcohol. May be used to refer to a person who is clean or sober, but not actively working the Twelve Steps. Refraining from or not participating in a particular behavior that may be considered harmful or not in alignment with one's own best interest or recovery program.

ACCEPT/ACCEPTANCE

Acknowledge, acquiesce, recognize/acknowledgement. Considered a spiritual principle meaning to recognize and/or resign oneself to a situation, occurrence, truth, fact, etc. To accept a fact does not imply that one agrees or is happy with it.

ACCOUNTABILITY/ACCOUNTABLE

Answerability, responsibility/answerable, held responsible. In recovery terms, being accountable means to honor one's word. Answering to another individual about personal actions, behaviors, thoughts, or feelings. Considered a spiritual principle.

ACTION

Deed, feat, movement. Task undertaken in order to achieve an outcome. Action implies putting effort into a thought or decision. When the word "action" is used in recovery, it could mean staying clean/sober/abstinent, attending meetings, talking and working with a sponsor, writing on the steps or doing step work, service work, changing behavior, etc.

ACTIVE ADDICTION

The time in an individual's life when he or she actively used mind- or mood-altering chemicals/drugs, including alcohol, or participated in a destructive behavior such as compulsive gambling, overeating, or the unhealthy use of sex or love. Also refers to the time period prior to getting clean/sober/abstinent when a person acted out in his or her addiction.

ADDICT

A person with a physical, mental, emotional, and spiritual reaction to the use of mind- or mood-altering chemicals and/or certain behaviors; one who is dependent upon a substance or behavior. A person who has the disease of addiction. A person who uses excessive amounts of any number of substances or participates in excessive behaviors that may be considered destructive to the self, which may include, but are not limited to, drugs, alcohol, food, sex, gambling, spending money, shopping, video games, or pornography. Characterized as being obsessive and compulsive. A term for a recovering member of certain twelve-step programs.

ADDICTION

Dependence, craving, habit. A chronic brain disease that affects a person physically, emotionally, mentally, and spiritually. The obsessive and compulsive use of a substance or participation in a behavior. Characterized by an inability to stop using or acting out, even after symptoms occur or there is a desire to stop. Usually results in negative consequences such as incarceration, hospitalization, etc. A self-centered or antisocial use of a substance or participation in a behavior that brings with it shame, guilt, paranoia, dishonesty, and negative consequences. Addiction affects people regardless of ethnicity, age, gender, sexual orientation, religious affiliation, economic standing, intellect, education, family environment, etc.

ADMITTED

Disclosed, acknowledged, confessed. To acknowledge a fact or truth. In recovery terms, to admit means to acknowledge one is powerless over addiction, his or her life is unmanageable, and recovery is possible. Many programs list the substance over which a person is powerless, such as alcohol, cocaine, gambling, etc. This is the first thing that must occur before someone can get and stay clean/sober/abstinent and grow in recovery.

ADVICE

Counsel, recommendations, suggestions. Giving another person a personal opinion or recommendation about what he or she should or should not do in a given situation or circumstance. Can be negative when unsolicited or not based on the personal experience of the advisor.

AFFILIATED

Joined, united, allied. Associated or connected to a group, business, facility, center, organization, etc. To be known publicly to be associated with a group, business, or organization. Affiliation can be direct or implied.

AFTERCARE

Continuing services or follow-up care offered by many inpatient addiction treatment and rehabilitation programs for patients who went through the facility. These programs often require "graduates" to attend continuing sessions for a predetermined length of time. Some of the topics covered in aftercare address reentry into society, employment issues, relapse prevention, and other recovery-related topics.

AGNOSTIC

Disbeliever, doubter, nonbeliever. Agnosticism is the intellectual position that the existence of God or other spiritual beings is uncertain or unknowable. An agnostic may believe there is a higher power of sorts, but does not believe in a traditional God or single omnipotent, conscious being.

AL-ANON/ALATEEN

A fellowship whose members share their own experience, strength, and hope with each other to learn a better way of life and to find happiness whether the alcoholic loved one is still drinking or not. Al-Anon's program of recovery is based on the Twelve Steps and Twelve Traditions of Alcoholics Anonymous. There are over 24,000 meetings in 115 countries.

ALCOHOL
Ethyl alcohol (ETOH) or ethanol produced by distillation or brewing. Consumed as a liquid (beer, wine, or spirits), is a central nervous system depressant which, when consumed in large quantities, impairs motor skills, judgment, and brain function. It is a drug and is potentially addictive; consumption causes intoxication and when consumed in large quantities and/or over time can lead to death.

ALCOHOLIC
A person with the disease of addiction that manifests as the excessive consumption of alcohol (beer, wine, spirits) and who has an abnormal relationship to alcohol. One whose life is adversely affected by his or her consumption of alcohol. Of a substance, relates to whether or not it contains alcohol. A term for a recovering member of the twelve-step program of Alcoholics Anonymous.

ALCOHOLICS ANONYMOUS (AA)
The first of the twelve-step programs, formed in 1935 by Bill Wilson and Dr. Robert Smith; its members' "primary purpose" is to get and stay sober themselves and help other alcoholics to become sober. A fellowship or society for people with the disease of alcoholism. The organization that owns the rights to the Twelve Steps of Alcoholics Anonymous and grants authority to adapt them to all other subsequent programs through express permission. *Alcoholics Anonymous* is the official name of the primary text used in the fellowship of AA. It was written by Bill Wilson and others.

ALCOHOLISM
A chronic disease that manifests as a reaction in the body to alcohol and a physical, emotional, mental, and/or spiritual need for alcohol. An alcoholic is said to suffer from and lives with the disease of alcoholism.

ALIENATE

Estrange, disaffect, set against. To separate from others. To create distance or isolation; may be done consciously or unconsciously, so as to conceal behaviors that may not be accepted by others and continue to engage in such behaviors.

ALTERNATE DELEGATE (AD)

A person elected by a regional service committee. This is a learning or training position. The AD will eventually assume the regional delegate (RD) position that carries the regional conscience on specific topics and/ or motions to the service conferences of various fellowships. Some of the twelve-step programs that have alternate delegates include Narcotics Anonymous, Alcoholics Anonymous, and Overeaters Anonymous.

AMENDS

Atonements, reparations, compensations. A key part of the twelve-step process, particularly Step Eight and Step Nine. To make amends is to correct an old wrong or change a behavior that had negative consequences. Amends may include a request for forgiveness for prior actions that may have harmed an individual or group. May be referred to as "ongoing amends" or "living amends," which is a continuing and concentrated effort to refrain from repeating a behavior that caused harm to another person or group.

ANGER

Fury, rage, antagonism. An emotional reaction to a stimulus, sometimes characterized by verbal or physical outbursts, other times marked by silence and "seething." Like all emotions, is neither "good" nor "bad"; however, its expression or repression may have negative consequences.

ANONYMITY

Namelessness, obscurity, vagueness. The state of being unknown, unidentified. A spiritual principle that serves several purposes in recovery, including:

- Promotes the ideal of humility by helping ensure that all persons in recovery are equal, with no member greater or lesser than another.

- Protects a person's identity by not referring to them outside of a group or meeting setting. (Since addiction is still poorly understood outside of the recovery community and many, even some of those who are new to the programs, consider it a moral failing rather than a disease, anonymity is often necessary to protect the jobs and reputations of those seeking recovery.)

ANONYMOUS

Unidentified, unknown, unnamed. See Anonymity.

ANXIETY

Nervousness, unease, apprehension. A feeling of being overwhelmed and/or overly concerned/worried by circumstances that may or may not be within one's control. Anxiety is often focused on events/circumstances that have not happened.

APATHY

Lethargy, indifference, lack of concern. Lacking interest in something or someone. To be indifferent to either one's own or another's feelings, experiences, or circumstances.

APPRAISAL

Evaluation, assessment, review. To look at oneself either through writing or sharing with a sponsor or support group.

APPRECIATION

Gratitude, admiration, fondness. To realize the value of a person or thing. To have an affinity toward a particular person, place, or thing.

APPROPRIATE

Apt, correct, proper. Behavior or language that fits a given setting. Behaving in way that is acceptable to another person, group, or society.

APPROVAL-SEEKING

Behavior geared toward obtaining the goodwill of another person or group. Needing, wanting, or depending on validation from another person to make one feel better about him- or herself, sometimes at the expense of one's own wants or needs.

AREA SERVICE

A committee meeting usually held monthly in which volunteer group service representatives (GSRs), subcommittee chairpersons, and administration members meet to discuss area issues; vote on motions affecting groups, the area, region, and world services of the fellowship; distribute literature; collect Seventh Tradition donations; and offer assistance to groups, etc.

ARROGANCE

Egotism, self-importance, conceit. Feeling or acting superior to others. Lacking humility about one's possessions, talents, gifts, or abilities and using them as a means of making other people feel inferior, less-than, or bad about their own lives.

ASSETS

Possessions, belongings, property/worldly goods. May be material or abstract, such as positive character attributes and aspects. Character traits or strengths that benefit recovery and the lives of others. May be referred to as part of a Fourth Step inventory process.

ASSUME

Presuppose, guess, imagine. To take a thing, person, situation, etc. for granted without proper investigation or knowledge of all the information pertaining to the thing, person, situation, etc. Assumptions may lead to resentments when an individual takes for granted that another individual will act a certain way and he or she doesn't.

ATHEIST(S)

Nonbeliever. Active or passive disbelief or non-belief in the existence of a God or gods. People who do not believe in a higher power that is a God(s), deity, or deities and who are in twelve-step recovery, may believe their higher power or "power greater than" is anything from the Twelve Steps, to their higher self, to the group, or anything non-material that is positive, uplifting, and greater than themselves.

ATMOSPHERE

Mood, ambiance, environment; as in "atmosphere of recovery." An environment that is conducive to open and honest sharing and that allows the message of recovery to be heard. An atmosphere of recovery allows those in recovery to feel that they are safe, even temporarily, from active addiction. Referred to in relation to a group or meeting's tone or environment.

ATTACHMENT

Connection, affection, bond. To have a connection to a person, place, or thing (may be positive or negative).

ATTENTION-SEEKING

Similar to approval-seeking; except that the attention sought may be negative or positive. May be expressed in actions or words.

ATTITUDE

Outlook, approach, mindset. State of mind or belief that is reflected in one's actions. A positive or negative mind set and way of acting that is usually a direct result of work one has done or not done on the Twelve Steps.

ATTRACTION

Pull, magnetism, appeal. A strong desire for something because of its appearance, attitude, or other appealing qualities.

AUTONOMY

Self-rule, self-government, independence. Able to make one's own decisions. To be able to govern as one wishes without outside direction, interference, or involvement. Acting in one's own interest. Also refers to Tradition Four in which "each group is autonomous." This tradition cautions that while groups may be autonomous, they need to ensure that their actions do not affect the fellowship as a whole.

AWAKENING

Developing, beginning, stirring. To wake from a state of denial about something and see it for what it really is. To identify a behavior or quality about one's self hitherto unknown; used in connection with spiritual as in "spiritual awakening" and often referred to in regards to the spirit. A realization of one's own actions and consequences, which may come about suddenly or harshly, as in a "rude awakening."

AWARENESS

Alertness, consciousness, attentiveness. A realization of truth in regard to some situation or idea. Considered the first part in the process of change; something one must have before being able to address addiction.

BAGGAGE

Personal belongings; past issues brought into present situations and current events. Fears, insecurities, and past harms that become ingrained into an individual's behavior and that influence his or her automatic responses to situations.

BALANCE

Stability, equilibrium, steadiness. Something an individual has when dealing with all areas of life in equal proportion and devoting an equal amount of time, effort, and concern to each area. Some areas commonly considered are work, emotional, mental, and physical health, spiritual well-being, and extracurricular activities or leisure.

BASIC TEXT

Another name for the primary text book of the twelve-step program of Narcotics Anonymous. The actual title for the Basic Text is *Narcotics Anonymous*. A recovery text written over a number of years by committees comprised of recovering addicts and designed to articulate the philosophy of this program. Also includes personal stories from recovering addicts. It was first published in 1982. There have been six subsequent editions released since then.

BASICS

Essentials, fundamentals, nuts-and-bolts. Program slang that refers to the fundamental or central actions one must take when entering a twelve-step program, which includes, but is not limited to, attending meetings, getting a sponsor, working steps, and being of service to others and/or the program.

BEGINNER

Novice, learner, apprentice. Also referred to as a newcomer, a person new to the recovery process, or one returning from a relapse. There is no commonly agreed-upon time frame for how long a person remains a newcomer or beginner, but someone is usually considered new or beginning based on the length of clean time more than how many steps he or she has worked.

BEHAVIOR

Deeds, manners, conduct. Behaviors can indicate a person's progress in recovery or lack thereof; can indicate a state of mind when words sometimes do not. Some behaviors advance recovery, others impede it; especially "old" behaviors that recall or might trigger a return to active addiction.

BELIEF

Faith, conviction, trust. A strongly held idea or concept; part of one's value system. The way a person or group views a concept or idea. Confidence in an idea, a person, or a group.

BIG BOOK

The primary text of the twelve-step program of Alcoholics Anonymous. The complete title is *Alcoholics Anonymous: The Story of How Many Thousands of Men and Women Have Recovered from Alcoholism;* it was first published in 1939 with four subsequent editions published since. After much debate among the founders, the name Alcoholics Anonymous was selected as the title of the book; the fellowship took its name from the book thereafter. The chief author of the Big Book was Bill Wilson; contributors and editors included Dr. Robert Smith (Dr. Bob), and Dr. William Silkworth, the "little doctor who loved drunks," though he himself was not one.

BLACKOUT

Lose consciousness, faint, pass out. A loss of memory or consciousness due to consuming excessive amounts of drugs or alcohol; associated with alcohol abuse and intoxication. Abusers of alcohol or alcoholics will often speak of having little or no memory of certain events because of being blacked out or in a blackout.

BOREDOM

Monotony, tedium, world-weariness. A feeling that time is passing too slowly because there is nothing stimulating to occupy one's attention. Feeling disinterested in current activities, unable to generate interest in or motivation to start new activities. May be the result of not having a hobby or interest in positive activities. Sometimes the result of depression; can be felt in early recovery when one has changed old behaviors associated with using/drinking before replacing them with new, recovery-oriented behaviors and activities.

BOUNDARIES

Borders, limits, margins. May refer to limitations, rules, or expectations of personal space, allowing others to know what is and is not acceptable in a relationship. Properly set and maintained, boundaries can protect a person.

BUGABOOS

An imaginary "something" that instills/causes fear, annoyance, or trouble in a person. Old feelings, ideas, concepts, or thought processes that may resurface, particularly in relation to feelings of inadequacy or insecurities about the ability to grow, change, or experience feelings of happiness or freedom.

CAME (TO BELIEVE)

Moved toward, arrived. A process or evolution; in most twelve-step programs refers to developing a belief in a higher power. This is something that may not happen instantly, but rather over time and through examples of that power's presence in one's life.

CARE/CARING

Be concerned, thoughtfulness; nurturing, protecting. To have and show concern for someone or something else by taking a personal interest in his or her or its well-being. May also relate to self-care, which would include taking appropriate action to maintain recovery, as in "to care for one's own recovery."

CARRY (THE MESSAGE)

Transmit, move, pass on. The message is recovery; sharing one's experience with the Twelve Steps is "carrying the message," conveying the idea that the Twelve Steps are an effective way to find recovery from addiction.

CHANGE

Modify, alter, transform. Becoming different or transforming through a process of working the Twelve Steps, going to meetings, listening to feedback from those with experience, and helping others do the same thing. A process of discovering the root of certain behaviors that have caused harm and finding new behaviors to replace them.

CHARACTER

Temperament, personality traits, the nature of a thing or person. The character of a person is often developed from personal and environmental experiences. In recovery terms, an individual's character can be repaired through working the Twelve Steps. Step Six refers to character defects that if not addressed can set the stage for relapse.

CHARACTER DEFECTS

Flaws, imperfections, part of human nature. Behaviors considered negative
and/or behaviors that cause damage to self or others. Manifestations of
addictive behavior that are commonly used in order to assist one in
finding people, places, or things that can bring immediate gratification.
Character defects may mask deeper issues that need to be addressed
if one is to stay in the recovery process. Actions someone takes that
result in consequences to him- or herself, as well as others. Not to be
confused with mere negative thoughts or feelings; character defects are
the personal negative elements that are at the root of maladaptive actions
and behaviors. There is no shame in possessing character defects as it is
part of human nature; the shame is in acting on them and not working
to change those defects.

CHARACTERISTIC

Quality, trait, attribute. Typical of a person or thing, distinguishing
him or her or it from other people or things.

CHRONIC PAIN

Physical distress, discomfort or pain/ache/soreness that lasts for longer
than six months and is usually the result of illness or trauma, although
the cause may sometimes be unknown. Chronic pain is often classified as
an illness in itself, emotional, as well as physical. The topic of discussions
in various twelve-step communities because it is frequently treated with
medications that under other circumstances might constitute a relapse
or cause addiction.

CLEAN

Unsoiled, spotless, dirt-free. In recovery terms, to be abstinent from
all mind- and mood-altering chemicals with the purpose of recovering
from addiction. Maintaining abstinence from a particular addictive
behavior with the purpose of recovering from that particular
manifestation of addiction.

CLEAN TIME

Words used to describe the amount of time a person has abstained from the use of drugs or addictive behavior. The term "sobriety" is used in Alcoholics Anonymous to describe an individual's continued participation in the program. Clean time is the preferred expression used in Narcotics Anonymous.

CLOSE-MINDED

Narrow-minded, insular, prejudiced. The opposite of open-minded. Rigidly disinclined to consider new ideas or concepts; clinging to already-established beliefs.

CLOSED MEETING

A twelve-step meeting that is only open to those who identify as suffering from the substance or behavior the meeting's fellowship addresses; e.g., a closed NA meeting is only for drug addicts, a closed AA meeting is for alcoholics, and a closed GA meeting is only for compulsive gamblers, and so on. Only alcoholics, addicts, or compulsive gamblers can share at these meetings; a member of the public who wants information about any of these fellowships can attend open meetings where all are welcome. Open meetings can generally be found in local directories or websites.

CODEPENDENT/CODEPENDENCY

Mutually dependent; relating to a relationship in which one partner is unhealthily psychologically dependent on another. One who is involved in such a relationship may be called "a codependent." There is a twelve-step program for codependents called CoDA.

CODEPENDENTS ANONYMOUS (CoDA)

A twelve-step fellowship whose primary focus is to help people develop healthy relationships. The only requirement for membership is a desire for healthy and loving relationships. Its recovery text is called *Co-Dependents Anonymous.*

CoDA was founded in 1986 in Phoenix, Arizona and has meetings in over forty countries with approximately 1,200 meetings in the US.

COLLAPSE

Crumple, fall down, disintegrate; have a breakdown of a mental, physical, emotional, or spiritual nature. May manifest as exhaustion, illness, or emotional outbursts such as extended bouts of crying or fits of rage. A mental, emotional, and/or spiritual collapse may be painful, but also can lead to a breakthrough needed in recovery.

COMMITMENT

Vow, promise, pledge. An agreement to perform a certain task, job, function, or fulfill a certain role or responsibility, either one time or recurring over a specified period of time. Often used in reference to service positions in recovery.

COMMITTEE

Group, board, team. A steering or business group comprised of trusted servants with a specific purpose, budget, guidelines, and elected volunteer positions, designed to carry out a specified task(s), organize or direct another group, or fulfill a stated mission. A group accountable to another body or group of people.

COMMON BOND

Mutual union/attachment. The connection between people in a twelve-step program is the disease of addiction or whatever substance or behavior the fellowship addresses, and the reason people come together at meetings is for the common purpose of recovery.

COMMON NEEDS MEETINGS

Meetings that are specifically designed for people with common issues above and beyond addiction and recovery.

COMMON SENSE

Coherent, sound, rational thought. Reasonable and practical judgment based on experience rather than study. Instinctual thoughts or ideas about a given situation or how to react. Not expected to be taught, but considered natural knowingness.

COMMON WELFARE

From the First Tradition of twelve-step programs; refers to the collective well-being of the fellowship and the reciprocal support needed in order for the fellowship to thrive. In other words, members could not find and/or stay in recovery if the fellowship was not in existence and the fellowship could not exist without its members.

COMMUNICATION

A message, announcement, or transmission. The practice of ensuring that both parties in a relationship understand each other by talking or writing with the intention of conveying a thought, feeling, idea, opinion, answer, directive, or request. A verbal or non-verbal expression of one's thoughts that may include sign language, facial expressions, body posturing, etc. It is considered an essential part of relationships and necessary for forming healthy bonds and/or intimacy with others.

COMPASSION

Care, concern, kindness. Having or displaying love or concern for another or toward oneself through words or actions. Showing consideration for another's well-being. Being sensitive to what another might be feeling. Having tenderness or being gentle with another and conscious of the impact that one's actions has on another.

COMPLACENCY

Stagnant, smugness, contentment. Being satisfied with a current situation while ignoring certain dangers. Being stuck in a rut or situation and not taking any action to do anything about it. Dangerous in recovery if the recovery process ceases or stagnates and the disease of addiction starts to gain more ground in the thought process or actions of the individual.

COMPLIANCE

Conformity (with rules), obedience, observance of rules. Usually a term used in treatment or clinical settings that refers to abiding by or agreeing with a particular facility's rules, laws, requests, and/or directives.

COMPULSION

Urge, impulse, craving. The uncontrollable urge or impulse to perform an irrational act, even with the sure knowledge it will be harmful. To fail to think an action through clearly or be fully cognizant of its consequences before performing that act. Spontaneous action not in the best interest of the individual. The constant and uncontrollable thought or incessant need to do something is the obsession that usually precedes impulsive action. Common obsessions include some superstitions, and/or fears of things most people consider harmless; common compulsions include nail-biting, self-harming, and the need to arrange items symmetrically. Compulsions often may be repetitive and physically damaging.

CONCEDE

Surrender, accept, or give in. To surrender after a struggle, argument, or denial. To begrudgingly acknowledge a truth. To lose an argument or a battle.

CONCEPTS (as in TWELVE CONCEPTS)

In recovery terms, the "concepts" refer to the ideals and suggested ways of how to perform service work in a healthy and recovery-oriented manner. Many twelve-step programs have incorporated the Twelve Concepts into their service structure. Some examples include The Twelve Concepts of NA Service (Narcotics Anonymous), The Twelve Concepts for World Service (Alcoholics Anonymous), The Twelve Concepts for OA Service (Overeaters Anonymous), and The Twelve Concepts of Service (Al-Anon/Alateen).

CONCERN

Worry, apprehension, alarm. To have or show a positive regard for someone or something. Can be positive in nature when an individual is being empathetic or helping one in his or her recovery; similar to compassion. On the negative side, can turn into worry, fretting, or anxiety over a situation or person because of a lack of knowledge about the outcome. Being overly concerned may lead to codependency.

CONFERENCE

Meeting, forum, discussion. Usually refers to business meetings that are held annually or biennially to make decisions regarding the literature of twelve-step programs/fellowships, discuss concerns or issues within the fellowship, elect board members/trustees, conduct fellowship business, and serve as a decision-making body of the collective group conscience of the fellowship. These conferences usually are comprised of representatives (delegates) from states, regions, and/or countries depending on the fellowship/program. Some examples include World Service Conference of Narcotics Anonymous, the General Service Conference of Alcoholics Anonymous, the World Service Business Conference of Overeaters Anonymous, Nicotine Anonymous World Services Conference, and Debtors Anonymous World Service Conference.

CONFERENCE AGENDA REPORT (CAR)

Also known as the CAR. Most common usage is found in Narcotics Anonymous; however, other twelve-step programs do generate a conference agenda for their service business meetings/conferences. A report sent out to groups and members of Narcotics Anonymous. The report lists all motions and discussions to be approved by the NA fellowship as a whole, including many recovery literature projects.

CONFIDENCE

Poise, assurance, self-belief. An assuredness or self-confidence that usually accompanies or is the result of working the Twelve Steps. Unquestioning faith or trust in the ability of an individual, group, idea, or concept because of personal experience, blind faith, or trust. Something that comes over time, but can be at times be confused with arrogance.

CONFIDENTIALITY

Discretion, privacy, secrecy. The practice of keeping private matters and/or issues secure or safe. To ensure that personal information is not shared with those it does not concern. Something expected from a counselor, sponsor, confidant, or friend.

CONFLICT

Clash, disagreement, contradiction. The inability to come to an agreement or make a decision.

CONFRONT

Face (as in come face-to-face with a person or situation), meet head-on, challenge. To tell someone something he or she may not want to hear about him- or herself and/or his or her behavior. Also refers to when a person must confront an issue/situation on a personal level.

CONFUSION

Perplexity, puzzlement, bewilderment. A state of uncertainty, feeling lost, being mystified, lacking a clear understanding; being overwhelmed with too much information.

CONSCIENCE (see GROUP CONSCIENCE)

Scruples, having a sense of moral awareness of right and wrong, ethics. Conscience constrains behavior, compelling individuals to act in certain (principled, ethical) ways and refrain from behavior that is unprincipled or unethical or may cause harm.

CONSCIOUS (CONSCIOUS CONTACT)

Cognizant, mindful, awake. In recovery, usually used in conjunction with the word "contact" and refers to a higher power, as in the Eleventh Step. Varies from person to person and is based on individual experience. Most often refers to an understanding or feeling that comes from being mindful of or having faith or believing that a higher power has one's best interest in mind and will take care of one's needs. In most twelve-step programs a conscious (contact) is usually achieved through prayer and meditation.

CONSISTENT

Constant, steady, dependable. To do something on a regular basis. The recovery process requires that one does some basic requirements on a consistent basis such as not using, attending meetings, and calling a sponsor.

CONTRIBUTION

Donation, gift, giving. To give financially or give of one's time to a cause or situation. In recovery terms, to give of one's resources (financial and/or personal as in sponsorship, helping to clean up a room after a meeting, doing service for the fellowship, etc.). The principle of contribution is discussed in the Seventh Tradition and referred to as "self-supporting through our own contributions."

CONTROL

Be in charge of, have power over, organize. To attempt to dominate, exert power or influence over, or to make decisions for another.

CONTROVERSY

Disagreement, debate, storm. Controversy exists when groups or persons are at odds or there are situations causing strife and contention. Some issues are more controversial than others. Controversy can occur when people have strong feelings or beliefs about a particular topic of discussion.

CONVENTION

A meeting, gathering, get-together. A gathering of program members held to celebrate or discuss recovery. Most twelve-step programs usually have some type of convention on a local, state, regional, and/or international/world level. Also referred to as "conference" in Alcoholics Anonymous. A convention can also be a standard, rule, or custom.

COPE

Handle, manage, address. The action of dealing with, addressing, or getting through a difficult situation whether the situation be illness, financial troubles, relationship issues, death of a loved one, etc.

COUNSELOR

Analyst, therapist, advisor. A person who has been trained or certified to counsel others in a particular area of concern, e.g., family and marriage issues, substance abuse, mental health disorders, debt, etc.

COURAGE

Valor, bravery, nerve. A spiritual principle showing strength through adversity or hardship. Attempting to persevere through one's fear in order to accomplish a goal.

CRISIS

Predicament, disaster, catastrophe. An emergency or critical situation. Many people find themselves in crisis because of the damage caused by their active addiction. A crisis can be medical, financial, marital, emotional, etc.

CROSSTALK

Term used in many twelve-step programs that refers to speaking directly to a person who has shared in a meeting and offering advice to them. Not waiting for a speaker to finish sharing and interrupting him or her to answer a question or give advice. Though there is no formal rule against it and formats vary according to each autonomous group's conscience, crosstalk is usually frowned upon and discouraged in most twelve-step meetings.

CULT

Usually refers to a religious group or sub-group of a larger religion. A faction or sect. Often isolationist and fervent in nature and prone to worshipping or following a single figurehead and/or object. Sometimes used to characterize twelve-step programs due to the devoted following of many of its members.

DAILY

Every day, once every twenty-four hours, once a day. As related to recovery, one must not use on a daily basis.

DEATH

The end of life; a cessation of existence in the physical world, loss of. Usually spoken of as one of the three likely fates of an addict who continues to use/abuse drugs and does not start recovery, the others being jails or institutions. There is also death of a spiritual nature as the result of using a substance or acting on a particular behavior in active addiction; however, this spirit may be rekindled through the application of the Twelve Steps.

DEBTORS ANONYMOUS (DA)

A twelve-step fellowship whose primary focus is to help people recover from compulsive debting. The only requirement for membership is a desire to stop incurring unsecured debt. *A Currency of Hope* is DA's recovery text that shares the recovery stories of thirty-eight DA members, what it was like before DA, and how the program helped them find serenity and prosperity.

Debtors Anonymous started in 1968 and was first called the "Penny Pinchers" and later "Capital Builders"; however, a few years of instability with meetings went by. After the fundamental understanding that the act of debting itself was the core of this disease, and the only solution was to use the Twelve Steps, DA began to grow. Today, there are over 500 meetings throughout the United States and in at least a dozen countries.

DECEPTION

Fraud, dishonesty, ruse. To be dishonest in order to cover up for certain actions or behaviors one feels shame or guilt over and of which one does not want to suffer the consequences. May also refer to the omission of certain elements/actions/behaviors of a situation or event. The result of a lack of courage to face the necessary consequences, resulting in more lies (deceptions), which compound upon one another and ultimately may lead to relapse.

DECISION

Conclusion, verdict, choice. To come to some resolution in one's mind that it is time to take a certain action. To choose to do something. In terms of the Third Step, it is referred to as an action rather than a thought.

DEFECTS (see CHARACTER DEFECTS)

Imperfection, flaw, fault. Sixth Step character defects are usually identified while writing the Fourth Step and when sharing that writing with a sponsor in the Fifth Step. In twelve-step terms, character defects may be negative behaviors from which people in recovery derive immediate gratification while causing pain or destruction to self or others. Defects harm relationships and keep an individual isolated. Isolation gives the disease more control over behavior and ultimately leads a person in a twelve-step program to relapse. Character defects stand in the way of developing a relationship with a higher power.

DEFENSE

Guard, protection, security. Most often used in conjunction with the psychological/behavioral term "defense mechanism," which means how a person copes with a specific occurrence and/or event. Active addiction often causes these defense mechanisms to be out-of-balance and/or exaggerated.

DEGRADATION

Disgrace, ruin, humiliation. An unacceptable state or condition of mind and body that usually comes as a result of losing what was formerly esteemed by a person in active addiction. May include material possessions, human relationships, attributes, etc.

DELUSION

False impression, misconception, illusion. An altered state of mind in which an individual believes that imaginary things are real or vice versa; distorted view of reality. Often accompanies active addiction.

DEMORALIZATION

Deflation, undermining, discouragement. Usually the result of compromising one's morals or principles in order to satisfy an immediate need be it drugs, alcohol, gambling, shopping, sex, etc. Engaging in acts out of desperation that would otherwise disgust an individual under normal circumstances. Most often experienced as a direct result of active addiction. Also refers to a feeling of discouragement or disenfranchisement as related to employment, relationships, etc.

DENIAL

Refute, rebuttal, disavowal. A key concept in twelve-step recovery, denial is the mechanism a person uses in order that he or she can continue to use addictively. An inability to accept reality and/or truth. Usually not conscious until external circumstances cause one to have an insight or an awakening. A person in denial may be fully aware of a destructive pattern of behavior, but may minimize or underestimate the impact of the pattern on his or her life. Until denial is overcome the individual most often will be unwilling to confront his or her addiction.

DEPENDENCY

Addiction, reliance, habit. Unhealthy need for a substance; mental or physical in nature that results in severe withdrawal that may be physical or psychological and often requires some type of detoxification. Emotional or other attachment to a behavior that provides a false sense of security and is therefore difficult to stop or break free from.

DEPRAVITY

Decadence, corruption, immorality. To be morally perverted, corrupted; lacking in virtues or principles. Indicative of the circumstances to which active addiction often brings a person.

DEPRESSION

Despair, misery, hopelessness. Feelings of extreme sadness, as in chronic depression, which involve a chemical imbalance in the brain often requiring treatment with medication. Symptoms of depression may be: lethargy, sadness, loss of motivation, loss of appetite, hopelessness, fear, etc. May be chronic or situational. Situational depression usually does not require medication and may be alleviated with the use of various forms of psychotherapy; it usually will pass when the situation causing it does.

DERELICTION

Negligence, delinquency, disregard. Also refers to neglecting things such as job or family responsibilities, etc. The word "derelict," for "bum," means one whose life is in ruins, who is abandoned or has abandoned a productive life and/or whose basic life needs are neglected or have been destroyed.

DESIRE

Longing, yearning, want. An extreme craving for something; to long or hope for. Often viewed in negative terms; however, in twelve-step programs desire is the only requirement for membership, as in "desire to stop using/drinking/gambling/eating compulsively/etc."

DESPAIR

The very pit of hopelessness, despondency, gloom. To feel anguished, lost, confused. Many twelve-step programs consider despair to be caused by not having a connection to a higher power. Also refers to how individuals often feel when they first arrive to a recovery program seeking help. A feeling one has when acting out on character defects and/or not working a program of recovery; the result of a negative or maladaptive behavior.

DESPERATION

Extreme anxiety, worry, abject fear. The feeling of "if I don't get what I need, I will die," usually coupled with some type of obsession or compulsion or the result of an obsession or compulsion. Most commonly associated with active addiction and typical of those seeking more of whatever substance/behavior to which they are addicted. In recovery terms, may relate to an individual who is desperate to get clean/sober or stop acting on certain behaviors.

DETACH

Disconnect, disengage, to separate from a person, group, thing, or place. Usually used in reference to removing oneself from something that may be deemed harmful, unhealthy, or dangerous.

DETOX (from DETOXIFY)

To remove or rid something from the body, usually in reference to toxic (poisonous) and/or addictive substances, particularly drugs and/or alcohol. Also refers to a medical facility dealing specifically with the removal of drugs/alcohol from the body in a controlled and medically-supervised environment.

DILEMMA

Predicament, tight spot, impasse. In recovery terms, dilemmas may relate to a crisis of conscience as a result of the conflict between old and new ways of life or old and new values and behaviors.

DIRECTION

Path, course, route. Instructions and/or suggestions on how to accomplish a task, arrive at a location, or put an object together. Also may be the suggestions given to a recovering person to assist him or her with staying clean.

DISAGREEMENT

Difference of opinion, dispute, quarrel. Disagreements do not have to be catastrophic. Friends can disagree and remain friendly.

DISAPPOINTMENT

Discontent, frustration, dissatisfaction. Feeling let down or sad about the outcome of a situation. Often occurs when expectations are not met. A feeling that may occur when life happens rather than what one would prefer to have happen.

DISCIPLINE

Order, restraint, punishment. Adherence to a code of beliefs and/or values. To hold oneself to a standard of actions, principles, etc. In recovery terms, discipline may refer to the consistent performance of certain actions such as praying, meditating, calling one's sponsor, going to recovery meetings, and not using mind- or mood-altering substances or engaging in maladaptive, compulsive behaviors.

DISCRETION

Good judgment, prudence, caution. Diplomacy, tact, the ability to make good choices. Discretion also can help an individual decide what to share with others in meetings and what is better shared privately with a sponsor.

DISEASE (OF ADDICTION)

Ailment, sickness, syndrome. The disease concept about the nature of addiction and alcoholism is recognized by the American Medical Association and World Health Organization, putting to rest the old idea that addiction is a mental or moral failing. In recovery, reference to "the disease" commonly means addiction—the threefold disease affecting body, mind, and spirit. It is chronic, progressive, incurable, and fatal if left untreated. The application of the twelve-step recovery model is considered one of the more successful treatments for the disease of addiction since it addresses the mind, body, and spirit of recovering individuals. Without any type of treatment, addiction is most likely fatal.

DISHONESTY

Untruthfulness, deceit, lying. Considered to be one of the more difficult practices to change for a recovering individual since dishonesty/lying is one of the characteristics of active addiction. Can be practiced by commission (lying) or omission (hiding) of the truth.

DISTURBING

Troubling, alarming, distressing. Something that agitates/disturbs the senses or makes one ill (on a physical, mental, emotional, or spiritual level) or causes discomfort. Causing stress or concern.

DIVERSITY

Assortment, range, mixture. In modern parlance, "diversity" refers to the myriad ethnic, religious, age, gender, economic, education, and other differences that mark the individuals in a group as distinct from each other. In addiction and in recovery, the entire spectrum of human experience is contained; no group is immune or exempt. Addiction can happen to anyone, and so can recovery.

DIVINE

God-like, Godly, heavenly. Recovery is often referred to as a God-given gift or a gift from a higher power. Also refers to a blessing or miracle believed to come from some ethereal source not of one's own making or doing.

DOGMA

An explicitly expressed belief, a manifesto, a creed. Often considered rigid and inflexible. A directive to act a certain way because it is believed some supreme being or religious practice necessitates it. In recovery, certain beliefs are very rigidly held by some groups, as if they are "carved in stone" and subject to only one interpretation. Some people, likewise, may be very rigid in their practice of their particular program of recovery.

DOPE-FIENDING

The action of manipulating a situation and/or person in order to get something. A slang term for doing something that is usually underhanded or even unethical, to get one's (addictive) needs met. Behavior seen most readily in those still in active addiction.

DREAMS

Aspirations, hopes, images. Also refers to the brain activity that occurs during REM (rapid eye movement) sleep. Something to strive and work toward. Many in recovery speak of "dreams that come true," in reference to those ideas or hopes that were lost in active addiction. Those new to recovery often speak about "using" dreams in which they use drugs or engage in addictive behavior. These "using" dreams can be very realistic in nature and cause distress. "Using" dreams can happen to anyone in recovery regardless of time in the program.

DRUGS

Medicinal or medical substances. Also refers to any number of mind-and/or mood-altering chemicals and substances, including alcohol. A habit-forming substance. May be prescribed by a health care provider or obtained illegally.

DRY/DRY DRUNK

To be free from alcohol. Abstinence from alcohol. Also refers to someone in Alcoholics Anonymous who is not actively working the AA program and is miserable and/or unhappy, as in "dry drunk."

DYNAMIC(S)

Vibrant, energetic, forceful. Able to change; motion. Various components or sides of a situation. All the parts of a scenario that make up its value; different qualities or complexities of a given situation.

EFFORT

Exertion, attempt, try. The act of attempting to bring about a desired effect. The act of trying as opposed to procrastinating, being lazy, or complaining about the current situation. Using physical or mental energy to do something.

EGO

The self, sometimes thought of as the personality, sense of self or the "I" of existence. The way one views oneself. Can refer to an exaggerated sense of self, an inflated view or opinion of oneself, or a destructive and hurtful view of self.

EGOCENTRIC

Self-obsessed, self-centered, inconsiderate. Focused on oneself, not considering others. Selfish. Considered a character defect by many twelve-step programs.

EIGHTH STEP

From the Twelve Steps (Step Eight); primary focus of this step is to write a list of the people (and institutions) harmed and become willing to make amends to all who (that) have been harmed. Also focuses on the individual becoming willing to change as part of the recovery process. These amends may be direct or indirect, including financial amends.

EIGHTH TRADITION

From the Twelve Traditions (Tradition Eight). A guideline stating that twelve-step programs should always be nonprofessional, but that their service centers are allowed to have employees called "special workers."

ELEVENTH STEP

From the Twelve Steps (Step Eleven); primary focus of this step is for the individual to use prayer and meditation in order to seek a "conscious contact" with a higher power.

ELEVENTH TRADITION

From the Twelve Traditions (Tradition Eleven). A guideline for twelve-step programs stating that public relations policies are based on individuals' behavior in recovery rather than actively promoting or advertising about their recovery. Also states that individuals should always maintain their personal anonymity in every medium.

EMOTIONAL

Poignant, touching, moving. To be moved by feelings rather than pure reason or intellect; expressive, sensitive, open, demonstrative. To have feelings, be affected by feelings, or to make decisions based on feelings. May imply coming from the heart (feeling) as opposed to from the head (intellect). Too much emotion may make a person seem overly dramatic; too little may make them seem heartless.

EMOTIONS

Sensation, passion; feelings such as sadness, joy, love, pain, fear, happiness, loneliness, guilt, etc. Any number of complex chemical responses stemming from the brain as a reaction to a particular situation, event, thought, etc.

EMPATHY

Identification, understanding, compassion. The ability to identify vicariously to another. A key component that makes twelve-step programs successful because individuals can relate to one another.

ENABLE

Permit, make possible, allow. To assist in accomplishing a task or maintaining a lifestyle.

The word "enable" forms the basis for "enabler," which defines individuals who, often believing they are helping someone recover, give the person money, food, shelter, or some other form of assistance.

The enabler invariably helps the person in active addiction to continue to use. Enablers are usually the parents, other family members, close friends, or loved ones of those who are addicted.

ENCOURAGE

Hearten, promote, cheer on. To support a person through a situation or an occurrence; to speak or act in a supportive manner.

ENDORSE

Approve, sanction, support. Financial payment, as in monetary sponsorship. Give a stamp of approval and/or back a thing (person, place, institution, political party, etc.).

ENTHUSIASM

Passion, zeal, fervor. A strong positive feeling and/or an expression of intense excitement for a particular idea, thing, person, etc.

EQUALITY

Impartiality, sameness, parity. Treatment of all people in the same manner. Also refers to equivalence, uniformity, and/or similarity.

ESOTERIC

Mysterious, cryptic, obscure. Unfamiliar, out-of-the-ordinary. Understood by a select few, e.g., a "secret society."

ETHICS

Values, principles, morals. A code to live by, moral standards, a set of guiding principles based on individual morals or the morals of a society or community; rightness of conduct either by an individual or organization. Many professional organizations have governing guidelines to ensure ethical conduct such as the American Medical Association, US Senate Ethics Committee, etc.

EXACT

Accurate, literal, to be precise and specific. To not be evasive or non-descript. In relation to the Fifth, Eighth, and Ninth Steps, to not be vague and to explain the specific nature of the wrongs an individual did.

EXAMINE

Scrutinize, study, inspect. The process of taking a thorough or detailed look at a thing, situation, or behavior.

EXCITEMENT

Thrill, enthusiasm; a feeling of joy, elation, or happiness deriving from a situation, action, or life in general.

EXERCISE

Implement, take action, put into effect. Also refers to working out (as in exercising or training). To perform some physical, mental, or spiritual action in repetition in order to build strength in an area, be it physical, social, mental, or spiritual.

EXPECTATION

Prospect, hope (for), anticipation. The state of wanting something out of a person, place, or thing. The belief that one will derive a certain benefit from a certain action. Hoping to get one's needs met in the way one wants; may cause a desire for unrealistic outcomes.

EXPERIENCE

Know-how, skill, understanding. The knowledge obtained through undergoing events. The accumulation of everything that has happened in one's past. Past occurrence. The process of actually going through something rather than hearing about it, reading about it, or watching it.

EXTERNAL

Exterior, outside, peripheral. Not integral to a person or a group.

FAITH

Assurance, confidence, trust. A reliance and/or belief (especially in God or a higher power). The act of having a conscious relationship with a higher power; to believe through experience or trust that the best or highest good will happen in one's life.

FAMILY

Ancestors, relatives, kin. A group of people who are connected, whether by blood, circumstance, or choice.

FANTASY

Flight of the imagination, unreality, dream. Something not based in reality. A daydream.

FATIGUE

Low energy, exhaustion, weariness. The state of being extremely tired or run down. Can be experienced on an emotional, spiritual, mental, and/or physical level. May stem from any number of physiological and/ or psychological causes such as poor eating habits, lack of proper rest or sleep, stress (physical/emotional/mental/spiritual), active addiction, withdrawal, etc.

FAULTS

Errors, wrongs, flaws. One's faults are not one's past actions; they are another name for the character defects one learns about after doing a Fourth Step with a sponsor. They are the negative qualities, such as greed, lust, or pride, that led to the actions that hurt others and oneself. The fault of "greed," for example, may have led one to theft or the fault of "lust" may have led one to cheat on a partner.

There is no one on earth without faults; our faults, some say, are what make us human. Sometimes our faults can lead us, through suffering, to do good; so no one need feel ashamed of discovering faults in themselves. The only shameful thing is to know one has faults and do nothing about them.

FEAR

Anxiety, terror, dread. The quality or state of being frightened, anxious, or scared. Fear can be of future events, outcomes (real or imagined) based on past harms, or projection of future harms. Fear is at the root of many other emotions, including anger. One may feel fear of losing what one has or not getting what one wants, and anger may be the result. Either emotion is dangerous to persons in recovery.

In recovery, the word FEAR is often used as an acronym; "**F**orget **E**verything **A**nd **R**un," to describe the attitude toward life's difficulties that persons in recovery may have taken in the past. A person in recovery may sometimes feel fear, but uses the tools of the program, including reliance on a higher power, to confront the life events that he or she would formerly have run from in fear. (The positive form of this acronym is **F**ace **E**verything **A**nd **R**ecover!)

FEARLESS

The state of being bold, daring, without anxiety or nervousness. The proper approach to one's Fourth Step inventory is to be "searching and fearless" when looking over past wrongs. One must not shrink from looking at his or her past actions, no matter how painful it is to do so; one must be fearless in facing them in order to continue on the path of recovery.

FEELINGS

Emotions, sentiments, sensations. Common examples include happiness, sadness, pride, embarrassment, bliss, joy, elation, gratitude, etc. Persons in recovery may not be used to actually "feeling" their emotions, having masked them with the substances or activities to which they were addicted. Avoidance of feelings is one reason many people give when asked why they began using in the first place.

Feelings may be overwhelming in early recovery as they begin to resurface, and even positive feelings should be shared, with a sponsor, in a meeting, or with a counselor or other support-system member. Feelings are nothing to fear, although it may feel as if they are when the feelings first emerge.

FEES

Charges, payments, costs. Money given in exchange for membership in a group or organization or a sum paid to obtain goods or services. Twelve-step fellowships do not charge any fees for membership according to their own traditions. Any donations members give at meetings are voluntary and are given to enable the groups to support themselves.

FELLOWSHIP/FELLOWSHIPPING

Camaraderie, association, comradeship. A group of people joined by a common desire, problem, interests, wants, needs, circumstances, etc.

Fellowshipping refers to the gathering with other people in a twelve-step program for social activities such eating, going to coffee, or for fun and recreation. Spending time with people in a twelve-step program outside of a meeting setting.

FIFTH STEP

From the Twelve Steps (Step Five); requires persons in recovery to admit—to their higher power, to another person (usually a sponsor), and to themselves—the exact nature of their wrongs. During this step, the person in recovery traditionally reads or recites his or her Fourth Step to a sponsor, but another trusted advisor, such as a clergyperson, may hear the recitation.

FIFTH TRADITION

From the Twelve Traditions (Tradition Five). A guideline for twelve-step programs stating that each group or meeting has one primary purpose, which is to carry the message that the Twelve Steps work to the person who still suffers from addiction in any of its manifestations.

FIRST STEP

From the Twelve Steps (Step One), this calls for the admission (acknowledgement) that a person seeking recovery is powerless over his or her addiction and that his or her life has become unmanageable. Said to be the only step that must be "worked perfectly." It is the basis and foundation for recovery, as the logical action flowing from admitting powerlessness over one's addiction is to abstain from the substance or behavior to which he or she is addicted. Only when one abstains can recovery begin to work in one's life. Only when a person admits to his or her "innermost self" that he or she is powerless can recovery begin.

FIRST TRADITION

From the Twelve Traditions (Tradition One). A guideline for twelve-step programs that states that the common welfare of the program should come first and that the recovery of the individual depends on the strength, stability, and unity of the twelve-step program. This is based on the belief that the program or fellowship must live, or its members will not. Therefore, the traditions were developed and adopted to ensure that what worked for the founders will be carried on to future generations.

FLASHBACK

Intermittent, unsought, and usually unwelcome memories of past experiences that can happen even after years in recovery. May be more common for those who have used hallucinogenic drugs. These can be frightening, but do not indicate that a person is about to experience a relapse. Like any other unusual feeling, a flashback should probably be discussed with a sponsor. If frequency and intensity is interrupting one's daily functions, a discussion with a medical professional to ensure there is no underlying physical illness might be a consideration.

FLEXIBLE

Elastic, supple, lithe. Having the ability to bend, compromise, or adjust to a changing situation(s). Also refers to a mental state that allows a person to approach the recovery journey with the open-mindedness and willingness required to succeed.

FOOTWORK

Skillful maneuvering, preparations, groundwork. The necessary work and actions associated with what one must do in order to work and stay in a program of recovery. Usually said in reference to going to meetings, getting a sponsor, and working steps. Might also refer to living life on life's terms, preparing to find a job by getting training, sticking to a budget to save money for things one wants, etc.

Many in recovery say, "I'm in the footwork business; my higher power is in the results business," to indicate their acknowledgement that even though they are responsible for doing the footwork of recovery (or of living), they are powerless over the results and leave those up to their higher power.

FORGIVE/ FORGIVENESS

Absolve, pardon, excuse. To relinquish resentments or grudges one has for another person, group, society, or concept.

Forgiveness is the act of or tendency to be forgiving and can be extended to others whether or not they apologize or make amends. To hold on to resentments or grudges without forgiveness hurts only the one who holds them; therefore practicing forgiveness is an important part of the healing process for most people in recovery.

FOUNDATION

Groundwork, base, underpinning. Firm footing on which to build a recovery program; establishing a connection with a regular meeting or group and with friends and peers in recovery, taking a service position, getting a sponsor, and working steps. Attending "ninety meetings in ninety days" is a time-tested formula recommended to newcomers wishing to establish a firm foundation in recovery.

FOURTH STEP (INVENTORY)

From the Twelve Steps (Step Four). Calls for a "searching and fearless" moral inventory. The particulars of working this step may vary according to fellowship attended. For example, some fellowships have people write a narrative/story or make a list or write in columns, but whatever format is followed, the Fourth Step inventory is a written assessment by a person in recovery of his or her own past deeds, revealing resentments, strengths and weaknesses, character defects, all aspects of his or her relationships, as well as assets. The point is to "inventory" one's character and to get rid of what is damaged and to see what needs to built up for continued healthy growth.

The Fourth Step is often approached with great fear by the newcomer, but there is no need for this. All the millions of people, all over the world, who have achieved lasting, long-term recovery through twelve-step programs, have taken Fourth Steps. While writing down one's past deeds might be embarrassing or even emotionally upsetting, it is never going to be as bad as having done those deeds in the first place! An understanding sponsor will be of great help in taking this step.

Old timers who have gone through the steps, including the Fourth Step, numerous times, insist that the Fourth Step is where true relief from the suffering of addiction begins.

FOURTH TRADITION
From the Twelve Traditions (Tradition Four). A guideline for twelve-step programs stating that each group and meeting should be self-regulating, except regarding issues that affect other groups, meetings, or the twelve-step program at large. Groups hold regular business meetings to autonomously determine the rules and format for their particular group's meetings and take votes, called "group consciences," to settle any issues. These only apply to the particular group itself; not to the program as a whole.

FOXHOLE PRAYERS
Adapted from the old saying, "there are no atheists in foxholes." The idea behind the saying is that a soldier in a foxhole (a desperate situation) will usually utter a prayer when enemy fire is getting close, even if he or she is not ordinarily religious.

A foxhole prayer is the sort of prayer people in active addiction utter in desperation after they are already in a bad situation (usually the result of behavior in active addiction such as incarceration, extreme illness, or hospitalization).

FREEDOM

Independence, liberty, autonomy. The result of living a life based in spiritual principles, working the Twelve Steps, and not being bound by active addiction. Those in recovery live lives that are truly free, though guided by the Twelve Steps and the principles of recovery, because they are no longer in bondage to their addiction or to the demands of "self."

FRIEND

Companion, comrade, ally. A person who provides love, support, companionship, or camaraderie. The friendships one makes in recovery are different in quality from the friendships one may have had while using. Often a person in recovery finds that the people he or she thought were friends have all vanished now that he or she is clean. Recovery friendships are based on a shared experience and common purpose, and encompass love, caring, and concern for one another's well-being.

FRIENDSHIP

Camaraderie, companionship, affinity. The relationship between two or more persons based on healthy love, trust, companionship, and camaraderie. A strong bond between people who spend time with each other, communicating and helping each other, and enjoying each other's company.

FUNDRAISING

Collecting and gathering money for a particular purpose. Many activities in twelve-step programs, such as dances, picnics, yard sales, bazaars, etc., are designed to raise money to support other services such as printing meeting directories, supporting helplines, or buying literature for hospitals and institutions.

GAMBLERS ANONYMOUS (GA)

A twelve-step fellowship whose primary focus is to help people stop gambling and to help other compulsive gamblers do the same. The only requirement for membership is a desire to stop gambling. Its members believe that gamblers of their type have a progressive illness and if left untreated, will only get worse and lead to prison, insanity, or death.

The first group meeting of Gamblers Anonymous was held on Friday, September 13, 1957, in Los Angeles, California. Since that time, the fellowship has continued to grow and groups can now be found throughout the world. Though the fellowship does not have a primary recovery text, there are several pieces of literature available. To help individuals determine if they are a compulsive gambler, a series of questions, known simply as "20 Questions" is offered. Most compulsive gamblers will answer yes to seven of these twenty questions.

Gam-Anon is a support fellowship for family and friends of compulsive gamblers.

GIFTS

Presents, donations, offerings given without the expectation of anything in return. Something bestowed on another with the intention of bringing joy, comfort, or uplift. May be material or spiritual and may include attributes or talents, as in "a gift for music."

"The gifts of the program can take us out of the program," is a recovery saying indicating that life in recovery can become so good that one may become "too busy," or feel "too cured" to attend meetings, meet service commitments, write, or otherwise work the steps, etc. These omissions are all indicators that a person is most likely on the road to relapse. One must always remember that unless recovery comes first, the "gifts of recovery" will not last.

GIVING

Generous, charitable, benevolent. The act of providing something to a person, group, or society without any expectation of return.

GOD

Divinity, supernatural being, deity. An all-knowing, ever-present supreme, supernatural entity/being. For many in recovery, their higher power may represent a return to the God of their childhood, or the word "God" may be a kind of useful shorthand for their higher power, easily understood by others to mean an all-powerful source of strength, comfort, inspiration, etc.

In twelve-step programs/meetings, the word God is often used to describe a higher power that is loving, caring, and only wants the best and highest good for the individual.

For some who have difficulty with the traditional concept of God, the word may be thought of as an acronym for **G**ood **O**rderly **D**irection, which is what the twelve-step program provides. A belief in God is not necessary for twelve-step recovery to work; although the steps do encourage that one finds a power greater than oneself.

GOD-AWARENESS

Awareness is consciousness, cognizance, or mindfulness. God-awareness is consciousness of a power greater than oneself. One awakens to this higher power when one realizes that recovery, which was once so elusive, is now a reality. The power that brought one to recovery is greater than and outside of oneself. This awareness or consciousness is developed and strengthened in recovery by the practice of the Twelve Steps.

GOD BOX or GOD BAG

A box or bag that a recovering person may use in order to pair a physical action with a spiritual one. The recovering person might write down on a piece of paper areas of concern, worrying issues, problems, etc. The person places the slip of paper into the box or bag to symbolize the "turning over" of the issue to a higher power. Placing items into the God box or God bag can be compared to saying a prayer.

GOD SHOT

An inexplicable, unusual, and encouraging happening (some might say a coincidence) that indicates to a person in recovery that he or she is being guided by a higher power. Something said to happen by the divine intervention or act of a benevolent being or cosmic conspiracy. Similar to, and used in the same way as, "miracle." Something that in the ordinary course of life does not usually happen.

GOD'S WILL

Will means resolve, determination, willpower. God's will refers to the intentions of the divine or higher power; the unstoppable manifestations of the mind of the creator. In twelve-step recovery, the recognition that following one's own will has led one to a life of unmanageability and pain is followed by the decision to follow the will of the higher power in the future, as best it can be ascertained.

Philosophers and theologians have spent centuries trying to discern and explain God's will, to no avail; however, most people in and out of recovery agree that actions that accord with God's will are those that are loving, benevolent, helpful, and constructive.

GOODWILL

Benevolence, kindness, care. Wanting and working for what is best for all involved, whether that means a person, group, community, or society. An inherent benefit of working the Twelve Steps and twelve-step programs is the development of goodwill toward others and experiencing the goodwill of others when it is directed toward oneself.

GOSSIP

Hearsay, rumors, scandal. Talking (or writing) about others in a negative manner, usually not in their presence; saying things one would not say about a person were the person present. Gossip may include sharing private information about others to cast them in a bad light (betraying trust) or spreading negative information, whether true or false, to gain some benefit for oneself. Sharing intimate details or secrets about others.

GRACE

A blessing or piece of good fortune. In twelve-step recovery, grace usually refers to unearned blessings bestowed by a higher power on those working the program. A gift from a higher power.

Grace also can mean physical elegance of movement, refinement, and poise, as opposed to awkwardness, embarrassment, and unease. Persons in recovery often speak of how the program has taught them to walk through life's problems with "grace and dignity."

GRATEFUL

Appreciative, thankful, indebted. Gratitude, or developing "an attitude of gratitude," is one of the most important tools in the twelve-step recovery toolbox. Since most people with addiction share a common feeling that "more is never enough," developing an attitude of gratitude represents a shift in the thought patterns of a person in recovery. Changing from "is that all there is?" one begins to approach life with a deep appreciation for the "little things" that was never there before.

Without gratitude for all that life offers, including both the things one perceives as desirable *and* undesirable, one is apt to become discouraged by the everyday challenges of life, and therefore vulnerable to the compulsion to use again. With an attitude of gratitude, life's "problems" can be seen for what they offer—opportunities for growth. An attitude of gratitude can make the difference between being a cynical, disconnected attendee at twelve-step meetings and being a joyful, connected member of the recovery community.

GRATITUDE

Appreciation, thankfulness, gratefulness. The feeling one has in recovery upon realizing the difference between where one could be in life and where one actually is.

Gratitude can be cultivated by noticing opportunities to appreciate the "little things" that one formerly took for granted or may even have regarded as annoyances. Writing a "gratitude list" every evening before one's daily inventory (Tenth Step) has helped many in recovery realize exactly how much they have to feel grateful for and the importance of maintaining this necessary attitude.

GRIEF

Anguish, heartache, misery. Extreme sorrow or sadness caused by the loss of something or someone important, as in the loss of a parent, loved one, or pet due to death, physical separation, divorce, etc. In early recovery, one may actually feel grief for the substance or activity to which one was addicted. It may be necessary to discuss this feeling with a sponsor, journal about it, or even, as some in recovery have done, write a "good-bye letter" to the substance or activity for which one is grieving.

GROUP(S)

Set, collection, assembly. In recovery terms refers to a gathering of people who regularly attend scheduled recovery meetings for the purpose of staying free from active addiction and helping others recover. Groups hold meetings at regularly scheduled times and locations; groups form the "fellowship" of twelve-step recovery. The single group a recovering person attends most frequently and for which he or she performs service work is usually considered that person's "home group"; there may be a formal enrollment sheet/book/list where home group members may list their first names, contact numbers, and their length of time in recovery in order to be of help to newcomers.

Attendance at group meetings is the most well-known part of twelve-step recovery, but it is by no means the entirety of recovery; in addition, there is sponsorship, service work, reading approved literature, and of course, step work, including writing and journaling. The group is where a person in recovery finds "experience, strength, and hope," as well as friendship with like-minded persons who share a common interest and goal—to stay in recovery.

Groups exist for all manifestations of addiction, for example Narcotics Anonymous, Alcoholics Anonymous, Overeaters Anonymous, Nicotine Anonymous, Sex-and-Love Addicts Anonymous, and Debtors Anonymous, to name just a few of the more well-known fellowships. There also are fellowships and groups for the families and friends of persons in recovery, such as Nar-Anon and Al-Anon. Contact information for these may be found in online or print telephone directories, as well as elsewhere in this book.

GROUP CONSCIENCE

The collective belief or decision of a group. It is not just a "group opinion" or majority vote, where the "loudest" voice can often sway others; the opinion of every member is sought, and all opinions are heard before a decision is made. Group conscience is a powerful spiritual concept; it makes it possible for people of diverse backgrounds and experiences to unite in furtherance of their common purpose: to remain in recovery and extend help to those who still suffer and seek recovery.

GROUP SERVICE REPRESENTATIVE (GSR)

A person elected to represent the group at area service meetings. The person who carries the group's conscience to area business, purchases literature for the group, learns about upcoming events, and carries this information back to the group. The GSR is the link between the group and other service bodies of the twelve-step program.

GROWTH

Expansion, development, progress. Growth may be physical or spiritual; an example of physical growth might be the increase in membership of twelve-step fellowships. Spiritual growth occurs as a result of working a program of recovery, including step work and service to others.

GUIDELINES

Strategies, guiding principles, rules. A set of directives to operate within, policies, by-laws, etc. These can be verbal, such as guidelines suggested by others who have had experience in the past, or written, such as the Twelve Traditions or Twelve Concepts.

GUILT

Culpability, responsibility, blame. The feeling of remorse for an action, behavior, choice, or lifestyle. Guilt, if not addressed in step work, can lead to paralyzing feelings of shame that may set the stage for relapse.

H&I (HOSPITALS & INSTITUTIONS)

H&I subcommittees are made up of experienced recovering people who take meetings/presentations/panels into facilities where inmates or residents are not able to attend regular twelve-step meetings.

HABIT

Routine, custom, pattern. A physical or psychological activity repeated often enough that it occurs without conscious thought. In active addiction it is the need for or dependence on a substance or activity. There are positive and negative habits; positive habits, such as regular meeting attendance or prayer and meditation, are often referred to as "disciplines."

HALF-MEASURES

Inadequate or ineffective actions, lukewarm or unenthusiastic attempts. Usually described as putting only half of the necessary required effort into what needs to be accomplished. Most persons in recovery say they must put at least as much effort into recovery as they did into using. That means full participation in the program—meeting attendance, step work, sponsorship, writing and/or journaling, and service work.

HALF-WAY HOUSE

A transitional living situation between a protected environment, such as a residential treatment center, and living fully and freely in society; may be a house, apartment, or building where people can live with others in recovery to help them adjust to life outside a controlled environment. May be co-ed or single gender, independently run or affiliated with a church, treatment center, or other organization. Also called "recovery houses," "sober-living houses," or "transitional houses."

HALT(S)

An acronym for the words Hungry, Angry, Lonely, and Tired; these physical and mental states often contribute to the desire to pick up. "S" is added for "Serious" to remind people in recovery to take their program seriously, but not to take themselves that way. (The acronym is then HALTS.) People in recovery are cautioned to avoid getting HALTS, as staying clean may be more difficult if they get out of balance by not taking care of themselves in these areas.

HAPPINESS

Joy, delight, gladness. One of the goals of recovery is to live life, "happy, joyous, and free." It is often remarked that if there were any happiness left "out there," people in recovery would still be using! However, persons in recovery know that active addiction only brings misery; never happiness. True happiness, joy, and freedom are found in recovery, in living a life free of the "bondage of self," in service to others, working the steps of the program of recovery, enjoying life to the fullest without the mask of addiction to stand in the way of life's simple pleasures, living with an "attitude of gratitude," and meeting one's responsibilities with confidence.

HARM(ED)

Damage, injury, wound. To hurt a person, group, community, society, organization, etc. with a behavior or action that is wrong or that causes damage; emotional, physical, or mental. In Step Eight, a list is made of "all persons we had harmed." In addiction, it is common to think "I only harmed myself," but in recovery, one realizes that many in one's life were harmed. Step Nine gives one the tools to repair these harms and requires that one do so, if doing so will cause no further harm to themselves or others.

HEAL

Restore to health, cure, repair. Settling differences, reconciling, rebuilding (especially relationships). Healing is one of the goals of recovery. The Twelve Steps offer a path to healing.

HELP

Aid, assistance, support. Twelve-step programs offer help in the form of fellowship, with the "experience, strength, and hope" of the group providing support and assistance to all those who seek it. Help is always available from one's higher power, if it is sought.

HELPLESS(NESS)

Vulnerable (vulnerability), weak(ness), incapable/incapacity. Without the necessary means, strength, or ability to take care of oneself. Helplessness is often confused with "powerlessness"; however, in twelve-step recovery, the distinction is made clear. One is not helpless over one's choices, one is not helpless over one's actions. One *is* powerless over substances and activities of addiction, over others, and over results. This is a subtle, but important distinction.

HELPLINE/PHONELINE

A telephone service that provides information about area/region twelve-step programs, such as meeting times and locations, to anyone who calls.

HIGHER POWER

A power greater than oneself; a God of one's own understanding. A key concept in twelve-step recovery. The only requirements be that this power is loving, caring, and greater than oneself.

HITTING BOTTOM

Reaching a point in the downward progression of the disease of addiction at which even the person who suffers from addiction realizes he or she has a serious problem. Varies from person to person; may be physical, emotional, material, or social. Considered the point at which active addiction ends, usually when the person has experienced enough pain, degradation, suffering, or consequences that he or she can no longer continue to use.

HOME GROUP

A meeting or group where members in recovery feel most at "home." Almost any twelve-step meeting can be a home group if people wish to join as members. Home group usually refers to the group or meeting that members attend regularly; vote on group, area, regional motions; help run the meeting; celebrate recovery anniversaries; and accept service commitments.

HONESTY

Truthfulness, integrity, sincerity. A spiritual principle that calls for truth-telling. It is possible to lie overtly (a lie of commission) or covertly, by withholding the truth (omission.) Twelve-step programs call for honesty as part of working a recovery-oriented program. Members in recovery should practice honesty with their sponsor, and, more importantly, with themselves.

HOPE

Anticipate, expectation, trust. The message of all twelve-step recovery is a message of hope and that "there is a solution." Hope is the belief that no matter how bad matters seem at present, there is a way for one's situation to improve; that all is not lost.

HOPELESSNESS

Desperation, bleakness, misery. To be without expectation of improvement. A particularly dangerous emotional state for those in recovery as it may lead to depression and unwillingness to participate in one's own recovery. Hopelessness can be combated by working the Twelve Steps, working with others in recovery, and being of service.

HORROR

Terror, repulsion, disgust. Considering one's past actions in active addiction may cause feelings of horror; working the steps and making amends for past wrongs is a way to overcome these feelings.

HOSTAGE

Prisoner, captive, detainee. Persons in recovery, when sharing, may refer to their partners and others as having been "hostages," so called because their well-being was subject to the feelings, needs, and actions of the addict. Even in recovery, it is possible to "take hostages," when one embarks on or focuses on a relationship, hoping for a "fix," instead of working a program of recovery, including working the steps, being of service, and working with a sponsor.

H.O.W.

An acronym for the way in which twelve-step programs work that includes the spiritual principles considered most essential to recovery: Honesty, Open-mindedness, and Willingness.

HUG

Embrace, enfold, hold close. Wrapping one's arms around another person, in greeting, farewell, or as a show of affection.

HUMBLE/HUMBLY

Unassuming, modest, self-effacing. The state of receptive self-awareness called for by the Twelve Steps, the attitude that fosters gratitude and receptivity to communication with a higher power.

HUMILITY

Unassuming nature, modesty, humbleness. Accepting both one's own assets and liabilities. A realistic view of oneself. Displaying grace and dignity without arrogance or conceit.

HUNGER

Appetite, need, craving. A physiological need for food or sustenance. As a verb, to hunger for something means to yearn, desire, or long for something that may be spiritual or psychological in nature, such as a hunger for love or friendship.

HURT

Injure, damage, wound. As a description, to be injured, in pain, or harmed; to feel pain. In active addiction, one has hurt many others as well as oneself. In recovery, one strives not to hurt others or oneself by words or actions.

RECOVERY
A to Z

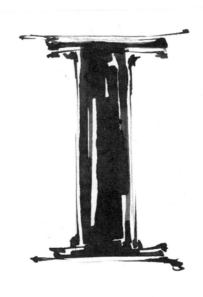

IDENTIFICATION/IDENTIFY

Naming, recognition, classification. To empathize with another's experience. In twelve-step recovery, to feel connected with another person, group, community, or society through seeing the similarities between them and oneself. The ability to understand, feel the same as, agree with, empathize or sympathize with another person, despite outward differences.

ILLNESS

Poor health, sickness, disease. Addiction is a disease that affects the mind, body, and spirit. It centers in the brain, and affects every part of the physical, emotional, mental, and spiritual well-being of the person.

ILLUSION

False impression, fantasy, daydream. Something imaginary appearing real, usually created in one's mind to support a fantasy or as the result of inaccurate perception of a situation. Addiction is the disease that tells the sufferer he or she doesn't have it; this illusion is often referred to as denial.

IMMATURITY

Infantile behavior, childishness, irresponsibility. The inability to handle situations with emotional, mental, or spiritual balance. Selfishness is one of the hallmarks of immaturity; the inability to delay gratification or think of others rather than solely of one's own feelings, needs, or desires. It is also one of the hallmarks of active addiction.

IMPERATIVE

Vital, crucial, very important. Certain actions are imperative in order for recovery to occur, such as abstinence.

IMPERFECTION

Defect, flaw, shortcoming. Imperfections are what make one human; striving to overcome them is what recovery is all about.

INCURABLE

Terminal, not curable, fatal. Something for which there is no known cure. Addiction is incurable; it can be arrested through the process of recovery, but one is never fully cured. Recovery is a state that must be maintained through the twelve-step process.

INDEPENDENCE

Autonomy, self-rule, freedom. To be on one's own, acting on one's own behalf. The state of being free from external influence or control or not being dependent on a substance or behavior. In its extreme, an isolated or alienated state.

INDIRECT

Roundabout, implied, veiled. Implicit in the Ninth Step; when making direct amends may cause additional harm to the injured party or to others, or when the injured party is no longer living or is unavailable, then indirect amends are called for; this is a way of making the wrong right that doesn't directly involve the injured party. Indirect amends may include living a full and useful life in recovery.

INDIVIDUALITY

Uniqueness, personality, distinctiveness. Personal attributes or beliefs held by one person. Unique qualities of an individual.

INFERIOR

Lower, lesser, substandard. Describes a feeling, whether perceived or imagined, of being "less than" another person or group. To feel oneself lacking in a quality or qualities, whether physically, emotionally, mentally, or spiritually. A perception of low worth or value.

INFORMATION PAMPHLET (IP)

Short pieces of literature (brochures) that are specifically focused on topics related to recovery; usually available at twelve-step meetings or central/administrative offices and treatment centers for free. Topics may include questions to determine whether or not one's use of a substance or activity is indeed an addiction, or may speak specifically to a population, such as youth, women, professionals, or gay and lesbian members of the community.

INHERENT

Innate, natural, intrinsic. A quality or value already implied, known, assumed, or possessed. An inherent quality is a base-level or fundamental quality that underlies all other qualities.

INJURE

Harm, damage, hurt. To hurt a person, group, community, society, organization, etc. with a behavior or action that is wrong or causes damage—emotional, physical, or mental.

INSANITY

Lunacy, madness, mental incompetency. Active addiction is a state of insanity and is accompanied by behaviors and attitudes of extreme mental distortion. A life in active addiction includes activities and attitudes that are clearly insane when viewed from the perspective of recovery.

INSIDIOUS

Subtle, covertly sinister, gradual and harmful (as is the disease of addiction). Capable of causing death or extreme destruction to oneself or others while seeming benign.

INSIGHT

Seeing what is hidden, perceptive, intuition. The ability to see clearly into the nature of a complex person, situation, or idea.

INSOMNIA

Sleeplessness, restlessness, wakefulness. The inability to sleep; often experienced with the withdrawal of chemicals during the beginning days of an addicted person's recovery. This form of insomnia usually passes as the substances are removed from the body. May be related to or associated with emotional distress.

INTANGIBLE

Vague, insubstantial, elusive. Indefinable or indescribable. Beyond reach. Something without a strong physical existence. An "intangible" is often associated with the benefits of recovery, because the life of the spirit is intangible, yet working a program of recovery is all about "building" this intangible, and yet, vital element of existence.

INTEGRITY

Truth, honor, reliability. Self-honesty, an ethical standard to live by. Doing the right thing for the right reason. From the idea of being "integrated," whole, having matching "insides" and "outsides," which means behaving and acting the same way in different situations (e.g., "behind closed doors"), regardless of the parties involved. Not participating in a behavior one would then be ashamed of revealing to others. Practicing the principles of the Twelve Steps in all one's affairs.

INTERDEPENDENCE

Mutual assistance, depending on each other, cooperation. A state of mutual and reciprocal reliance between entities. Characteristic of the sponsor-sponsee relationship, in which each depends upon the other for support and ongoing recovery.

INTERVENTION

Intercession, involvement, coming between. The formal process of "coming between" a person in active addiction and his or her addiction. A confrontation between the person with addiction and individuals affected by his or her addiction, often mediated by trained professionals, with expertise in conducting and directing these interventions; they are called interventionists.

INTIMACY

Familiarity, closeness, understanding. Something of a personal or private nature, something that is familiar. Sharing personal information with another person. Often characterized by love or affection, and sometimes sex, although sex may occur without true intimacy. Intimacy often happens through working steps with a sponsor and sharing things with him or her that one might not feel safe revealing to a group or in public.

INTOLERANT

Narrow-minded, bigoted, lacking in acceptance. Unable or unwilling to accept (another person or thing, such as a way of life). Not respecting that which is different from oneself. Lacking patience or understanding.

INTOXICATION

The state of being under the influence of alcohol or other mood-altering drugs; usually used in reference to alcohol consumption. The word "toxic" contained within the word intoxication means "poisonous."

May also refer to being intensely overjoyed or excited to the point that a person becomes irrational.

INVENTORY

List, account for, record. In recovery terms, an inventory is a part of both the Fourth and Tenth Step processes, calling for the listing and writing about assets, defects of character, fears, resentments, etc., to discover the exact nature of one's past wrongs/behavior patterns.

Many different acceptable inventory formats are in use in the various fellowships; one's sponsor can suggest a format, and this part of the program should be done under the supervision and direction of a sponsor. The inventory is not done merely to find fault or affix blame, but as an inventory would be done in business; to "uncover, discover, and discard" items that are unusable or unwanted, so that they can be replaced with positive qualities.

ISOLATION

Remoteness, seclusion, aloneness. The act or practice of separating from others, remaining alone or apart. Isolation is a major factor in addiction; active addiction is often marked by using in isolation from others or remaining aloof so one's use of substances or activities is not detected. Isolation may also be the result of paranoia induced by any number of substances.

In recovery, isolation, whether deliberate or unintentional, often precedes a relapse. Failing to avail oneself of the support of the fellowship, skipping or abandoning meetings altogether, or avoiding contact with one's sponsor are all danger signals, and one must monitor one's own behavior to ensure that isolation is not becoming a renewed habit.

ISSUE

Matter, topic, subject. In recovery, a question, concern, or problem. May be a behavior or habit that comes up repeatedly and causes pain and discomfort, or keeps an individual from moving on to another level in his or her recovery. Issues may revolve around many topics; abandonment, fear of intimacy, finances, body-image, lifestyle, loss of a loved one; all these (and many more) are issues that can impact one's recovery.

JACKPOT

Bonanza, top prize, win all. Originally a positive term from gambling, meaning to win the entire "pot" or "pool." Jackpot has recently acquired an additional negative meaning, often heard during twelve-step meetings, when a speaker describes having landed in a "jam," bind, or crisis that may involve jail time, divorce, or financial hardship, etc.

JOURNALING

The practice of writing thoughts, feelings, or concerns down on paper (in a journal) in an attempt to work on or process them. Journaling is a beneficial and widely used tool in recovery as an aid to self-knowledge and increasing insight. Continued journaling throughout the course of one's recovery will provide documentary evidence, if any is needed, of the changes one experiences during the journey of recovery.

JOURNEY

Voyage, trip, expedition. A process, as opposed to an event. Recovery is often compared to a journey, a trip one takes through life, passing through stages along the way, from the depths of despair to the higher ground of a life lived in serenity.

JOY

Happiness, elation, bliss. A life lived in recovery can provide one with the ability to extract joy from simple things; family, friendship, and the satisfaction of knowing one is a useful and contributing member of society.

JUDGE/JUDGING

Evaluate/evaluating; decide/deciding; conclude/concluding. Judging others can be a character defect in recovery when it becomes the act of finding faults, flaws, or imperfections in others for the purpose of putting them down. One's focus in recovery should be more on improving oneself, not on tearing others down.

JUDGMENTAL

Hypercritical, condemnatory, disapproving. Engaging in the kind of criticism of others described above, estimating them as "less than" in order to make oneself feel or seem superior.

KEY TAGS

Colored plastic key chains given out at recovery meetings for various, incremental lengths of clean-time. Different twelve-step programs have different sets of key tags to designate different lengths of abstinence; usually newcomer (24-hours), 30-, 60-, and 90-days, six-, nine-, and eighteen months, plus one-year and multiple years. Some fellowships give out plastic or metal "chips" or "tokens," rather than key tags, to celebrate lengths of time in recovery.

KINDNESS

Gentleness, compassion, thoughtfulness. Kindness is a virtue, in recovery as in life, and enables a person in recovery to be available to help others, whether newcomers or "old-timers," to achieve the common purpose of the twelve-step fellowship.

KNOWLEDGE

Facts, data, awareness. A word in the Eleventh Step that refers to gaining or learning information about a higher power's will for one, often gained through experience in recovery.

LEADER(S)

Director(s), chief(s), guide(s). A person who possesses certain qualities that inspire others or invoke enthusiasm; people to whom others look for guidance, direction, hope, inspiration, and comfort or who provide direction and/or suggestions. Leaders of this type lead by example, not because they hold an official office.

LEADERSHIP

The act or practice of being a leader; the act of behaving in such a way as to provide direction, guidance, or inspiration that other people choose to follow.

LEGAL DRUGS

Prescribed medications and over-the-counter medication (OTC medication). Although legal, these substances can be mind- and mood-altering. Those in recovery need to practice extreme caution when taking prescribed or OTC medication and stay in close contact with their sponsor, especially if the prescribed medication is an opioid or painkiller.

Alcohol is considered a legal drug.

LETTING GO

The practice of turning a problem over to one's higher power. This can be described as practicing the Third Step. "Let go and let God," is one expression of this principle.

LIABILITIES

Weaknesses, problems, burdens. Actions, attitudes, or behaviors a person resorts to in addiction or in addictive behavior that keep him or her separated from others or from his or her higher power. In recovery, liabilities may also be referred to as character defects.

LIMITATION(S)

Restriction(s), constraint(s), inadequacy(ies). Reaching the end of one's abilities or capacity. A person in recovery who is spiritually fit, that is, practicing twelve-step recovery in all his or her affairs, should have very few limitations on what he or she can do or where he or she can go in recovery.

LISTEN

Take note, pay attention, to hear. An active part of the communication process between two or more people takes place when one listens to what another is saying and processes and interprets that information. In early recovery, newcomers especially are advised to "learn to listen, then listen to learn."

LITERATURE

Writing, text, prose. In twelve-step programs, "recovery literature" refers to books, workbooks, information pamphlets, or service manuals that have been approved by the World or General Service Organizations having to do with the nature of addiction and recovery. Many people in recovery who live in remote locations where there are few meetings or who are incarcerated, hospitalized, or institutionalized rely on the message contained in the basic texts of their fellowships for comfort and support when another person in recovery is not available.

LONELINESS

Isolation, aloneness, friendlessness. A painful and unpleasant feeling, common among persons in active addiction, and sometimes among those in recovery. Usually a deep feeling of sequestration, isolation, or seclusion due either to actual physical separation from others or from a feeling of being disconnected from others on an emotional, mental, or spiritual level.

LOST

Missing, gone, disoriented. In the metaphysical or philosophical sense, to not know where one is or where one is going. Mentally, to be confused or disoriented. Spiritually, a feeling of being out of place, different from others, a beat behind, or disconnected from a higher power; not knowing what will happen, not being familiar with practices, customs, etc. The feeling of being lost is best overcome by increased participation in the fellowship, by meeting attendance, and service work.

LOVE

Devotion, care, concern. The willing extension of one's self for the spiritual, emotional, mental, and physical betterment of another. The love that is felt and practiced in twelve-step fellowships is real and enduring. It is the sort of "brotherly" or "sisterly" love that is expressed in very practical ways; by calling others on the phone, by giving a ride to a newcomer without a car, by inviting a person who is alone to share a meal. This love is the missing ingredient in the lives of most persons in active addiction and may be replaced in full by membership in a twelve-step fellowship.

LYING

Deceiving, double-dealing, tricking. Lying may be by omission (not telling something or not telling *all* about something) or by commission (actually creating false information). Active addiction is a life built on lying. Recovery is a life built on honesty—with oneself, a higher power, and others.

MAINTAIN

Preserve, uphold, continue. Regular effort one must expend in order to continue on a current path. To do the work necessary on an ongoing basis in order to continue to grow in one's recovery.

MAINTENANCE

The process of preserving, upholding, or continuing something. Expending effort on a regular basis to maintain one's recovery. To participate regularly in the recovery process and all that that entails; attending meetings, making sponsor contact, reading recommended literature, writing and working steps, being of service, etc.

MEDICATION

In recovery terms, usually refers to any medicine prescribed by a medical professional legally authorized to write prescriptions. Doctors, psychiatrists, and nurse-practitioners may prescribe medication to treat illnesses, ailments, or injuries. Medication may either be prescribed to alleviate symptoms or to cure an illness.

MEDITATE/MEDITATION

Reflect, contemplate, ponder. To attempt to focus the mind on one thought, to relax the mind. A centering, peaceful, serene, or grounding exercise. There are many different meditation techniques; meditation is a very personal process, unique for each person. Some people use breathing exercises, visualizations, mantras (repeated words or phrases), or other specific techniques, while others may simply sit in silence and attempt to concentrate on their own breath. While there are many different religions and programs that teach specific practices, ultimately, it is something that is adapted by the individual to fit his or her needs.

MEDITATION BOOK

A daily reinforcement of recovery in a condensed, easy-to-read format. These books give a recovering person a positive thought to focus on as they go about their recovery each day. There are many different types of meditation books, geared toward particular issues or groups, including addicts, alcoholics, compulsive gamblers, men, women, codependents, adult children of alcoholics, those suffering from mental illness, abuse survivors, etc.

MEETING

Assembly, gathering, get-together. Two or more people coming together for the purpose of recovery from their addiction constitutes a recovery meeting. A setting in which people can meet for the purpose of sharing experience, strength, and hope with one another. Twelve-step meetings take place at regularly scheduled locations and times and are listed in a schedule/meeting list and are usually populated with members who attend on a regular basis and perform service commitments that ensure the meeting is run smoothly and properly. Formats vary by program and community, but follow a basic pattern.

Common formats include: speaker meetings, open discussion, literature studies, step studies, topic discussion, etc. Some meetings may be more specialized within a particular program.

MEETING ETIQUETTE (See section on Meeting Etiquette, page 153.)

Decorum, manners, protocol. The etiquette, or acceptable behavior, for persons attending meetings varies in different twelve-step programs and among various groups and meetings within each particular program; however, certain activities are universally discouraged. Examples of discouraged behaviors may include "cross-talking," talking with one's neighbors, using communication devices like cell phones during meetings, bringing children or others to a closed meeting, or leaving one's seat noisily and/or repeatedly. Etiquette can be easily learned by using common sense and by visiting different groups.

MEMBER

Constituent, associate, affiliate. A person who identifies as being a part of a twelve-step program. The Third Tradition in various programs states that the "only requirement for membership is a desire to stop:" using, drinking, or participating in certain activities, but it does not insist that one must be clean, sober, or abstinent before becoming a member or even after attending several meetings.

MEMBERSHIP

The state of belonging to, participating in, or signing-up for a group, fraternity, fellowship etc., such as a twelve-step fellowship. Requirements and stipulations for membership depend on the type of group, but it is generally accepted within most fellowships that membership starts when one says one is a member.

MENTAL ILLNESS

Insanity, lunacy, psychosis. Lack of mental health or clarity, mental suffering. The state of being clinically depressed or suffering from other afflictions, such as schizophrenia, dementia, etc. that go beyond the scope of twelve-step programs, which are designed to address the disease of addiction. Mental illnesses usually require attention from a medical doctor or psychiatrist.

MESSAGE

Meaning, point, significance. The message of recovery is the mission statement of a fellowship that "there is a solution," and recovery is possible through working the Twelve Steps.

MIRACLE

Phenomenon, marvel, wonder. Any event apparently beyond human powers and ordinary understanding of the laws of nature. Any happening so unusual as to have been thought impossible, such as a mother suddenly having the strength to lift a car that had run over her child, to an addict getting one day clean. Usually attributed to some sort of divine providence or intervention from a higher power.

MODERATION

Temperance, restraint, self-control. Balance between extremes. To engage in an activity within limitations, not acting or doing something in excess. To find a balance, a rhythm, a healthy gauge. Recovery teaches moderation, or balance, in all things and all aspects of life, including the mental, physical, emotional, and spiritual.

MONEY ISSUES

Problems relating to money; financial issues; whether related to over-spending, under-earning, or failure to establish or follow a budget or pay bills.

MOOD-ALTERING

Anything that changes or alters one's disposition or frame of mind. Refers to any drug, including alcohol, consumed by an individual to effect a change in, or alter, consciousness, feelings, or emotional state; may include other substances or activities (manifestations of addiction) that a person might use, such as food, caffeine, nicotine, shopping, sex, etc.

MORAL(S)

Values, ethics, principles. A code of beliefs influencing a person's own behavior. Morals relate to a personal understanding of right and wrong. Although each individual person must develop his or her own particular moral code, there are generally accepted moral conventions that have throughout time been consistent across all cultures, e.g., that it is wrong to kill or steal from others.

MORAL INVENTORY

The listing of past actions, resentments, assets, and liabilities in an attempt to determine the exact nature of wrong and right behavior and to reveal character defects that one will ask a higher power to remove in the Seventh Step. Part of the Fourth Step in a twelve-step recovery program.

NAR-ANON

A twelve-step fellowship whose primary focus is to help relatives and friends who are concerned about the addiction or drug problem of another. The Nar-Anon program is adapted from the Twelve Steps of Narcotics Anonymous.

NARCOTICS ANONYMOUS (NA)

A twelve-step recovery program, adapted from Alcoholics Anonymous (AA), to address the disease of addiction. To emphasize that it is a "we" program, and to differentiate from AA's Twelve Steps, the first eleven steps begin with the word "we" and reference to alcohol is changed to "our addiction" in the First Step. Formed in July 1953 in California, with literature translated into thirty-six languages and meetings in more than 134 countries around the world. The founder of Narcotics Anonymous is considered to be an addict named Jimmie K.

NATURE

Environment, life, character. The natural world or the basic, elemental character and temperament of a person or a thing. The nature of something is what it *is* fundamentally. Discovering one's own nature would include discovering the causes or roots of problems that are not attributable to any outside person or any event, but that are characteristic solely of oneself.

NAWS

Narcotics Anonymous World Services, or NAWS, is the non-profit corporation for the fellowship of Narcotics Anonymous. The World Service Office (WSO) is the primary headquarters, located in Chatsworth, California. WSO is an office where Narcotics Anonymous literature can be purchased and is the hub for fellowship development services and communication.

NEWCOMER(S)

A person (or persons) in early recovery; specific length of time one is considered a newcomer varies depending on the fellowship and geographic location, as well as other factors, including behavior and attitude. The main focus during this stage of recovery is on such activities as meeting attendance on a daily basis, reading recovery literature, building a relationship with a sponsor and a support group, and joining a home group; all referred to as "building a foundation."

NINTH STEP

From the Twelve Steps (Step Nine); it requires the recovering person to make amends to all people he or she has harmed, except when doing so would cause further injury to the injured party or others.

NINTH TRADITION

From the Twelve Traditions (Tradition Nine). A guideline for twelve-step programs stating that twelve-step groups and members should never be under external or internal management or control ("…ought never be organized"), but that those groups may form service bodies and committees that are directly responsible to the groups that are served.

NON-AFFILIATION

Not closely connected. To have no direct association, in name or function, with an organization, group, association, company, or individual outside of the twelve-step program, such as a treatment center or hospital, although the twelve-step program may cooperate with such institutions or hold meetings on its premises.

NON-DISCRIMINATION

To neither exclude nor include members because of some factor such as race, creed, religion, lack of religion, sexual orientation, or any held values or opinions.

NON-PROFESSIONAL

A person (worker) who is not paid to provide counsel, nor is he or she a doctor or therapist bound by a Hippocratic oath. A person who is not a professional in a specific field; without licensure or degree.

OBSESSION

Fascination, passion, mania. An intense, insistent, constant drive, need, or fixation (fixed idea), desire, all-one-can-think-of, constant thinking about a specific topic, idea, problem, person, or situation to the exclusion of all else. Continual thoughts of using drugs or acting out on a behavior. An intense feeling that one must use drugs or act out on a behavior to satisfy the obsession, no matter what the consequences are.

OLD TIMER

A recovering person with significant clean time/sobriety/abstinence; specific time depends on geographic location, particular twelve-step program, and on the general "age" of the local recovery community. An old timer is a person with significant experience in a twelve-step program who has spent a great deal of time abstaining from a substance or behavior and living "life on life's terms," free from active addiction. People with substantial clean time/sobriety/abstinence who have more experience dealing with life situations and have a greater distance between themselves and active using than newcomers.

OMNIPOTENT

Invincible, all-powerful, almighty. This word is usually associated with the God of Western religion, and many in twelve-step recovery understand their higher power to be omnipotent. Along with omnipotence, the higher power is also considered to possess omniscience (all knowledge) and omnipresence (universal presence).

OPEN MEETINGS

Twelve-step meetings that welcome persons who are not members of that particular fellowship, including family members or members of the general public who may be interested in seeing how the meetings are run or how the program works. Sometimes a person who is not quite ready to enter a twelve-step program as a member will attend open meetings to "test the waters."

OPEN-MINDEDNESS

A non-judgmental attitude, tolerance, permissiveness. Considered a spiritual principle in practicing the Twelve Steps. The quality of accepting others' right to their own feelings and opinions, listening respectfully to other opinions, ideas, beliefs, or suggestions, and being open to the possibility that those ideas have merit. A willingness to listen to another person in recovery and attempt to hear what that person has to share. The humility necessary to listen to opposing points of view.

OPINION

Estimation, belief, judgment. A judgment or personal, subjective analysis of a topic, issue, situation, etc. What a person or group may feel, believe, or value about a certain situation, topic, etc. Opinions are often based on feelings, beliefs, fears, or on past experiences rather than on knowledge or facts.

ORDER

Stability, organization, tidiness. Also refers to sequence, ranking, classification, as in "the steps are in order for a reason." The absence of chaos, the opposite of disorganization and disorder.

OUTSIDE ENTERPRISES

Enterprises are businesses, business activities aimed at profit, or organizations. "Outside enterprises" are organizations, associations, companies, or political entities that are not connected or affiliated with twelve-step programs. Ideally, twelve-step program members should not share about politics, religion, or other "off-topic" subjects at meetings, but should confine their comments to the common problem that the meeting addresses, rather than "outside enterprises."

OUTSIDE ISSUE(S)

Matters or concerns outside the realm of addiction and recovery. There are differing opinions about what these issues might be. Many believe that mentioning other fellowships (such as by discussing drugs in an AA meeting or alcohol in a GA meeting), talking about politics, religion, the need for medication in recovery, etc. might fall into this category. Others believe this term refers to the need for the twelve-step fellowship as a whole to avoid endorsing or expressing any opinion on issues that do not concern the program itself.

OVEREATERS ANONYMOUS (OA)

A twelve-step fellowship whose primary focus is to help people recover from compulsive eating. OA is not just about weight loss, gain or maintenance or obesity or diets. It addresses physical, emotional, and spiritual well-being. Its recovery text is called *Overeaters Anonymous*.

OA was cofounded by Rozanne S and Jo S in 1960. These two members, along with another compulsive overeater, Bernice S, held the first OA meeting in Los Angeles, California on January 19, 1960. Today there are 6,500 OA groups in over seventy-five countries. It is estimated that there are approximately 54,000 members worldwide.

PAIN

Soreness, aching, hurt. Suffering, whether physical, mental, or emotional, from an affliction or due to having been hurt or injured. Anguish over a given situation or set of circumstances. Emotional pain is believed to be behind much more active addiction than physical pain, although persons suffering physical pain for extended periods of time (chronic pain) are in danger of becoming addicted to opioid painkillers or of "self-medicating" with other drugs or alcohol, and may need to enter their own program of recovery to address both their pain issues and their addiction.

PARADOX

Contradiction, inconsistency, irony. Two ideas that in theory cannot coexist or two juxtaposed concepts that appear opposite; expressed in twelve-step quotes such as "surrender to win."

PARALLEL

Corresponding, equivalent, running-alongside. A resemblance or congruence. Railroad tracks are often cited as an example of things that are parallel.

PARANOID

Fearful, mistrustful, suspicious. Suffering from fear of real or imaginary situations or enemies or feeling that other people are out to harm one. Can be and is often a result of excessive use of mind- and mood-altering chemicals or extreme trauma or abuse. A fear or expectation that one is going to be hurt or deceived by others; a profound distrust of other people or feeling as if one is being conspired against.

PATIENCE

Staying power, endurance, lack of complaint. A spiritual principle. The state of being tolerant with and of others, the ability to wait, the ability to allow time to pass before making a decision or taking action. Doing the footwork necessary for a result without expecting immediate gratification. Allowing another person to experience his or her feelings; it can be a form or demonstration of love. A person practicing patience does not react in anger when something does not turn out as he or she may have desired.

PATTERN(S)

Model, prototype, plan used in making things. A system of behavior or a series of behaviors that lead to similar outcomes. A *modus operandi*, hidden agenda, habitual behavior, or chronic, repeated reaction to different life events or situations. A person in recovery usually will uncover behavior patterns after completing a Fourth Step inventory.

PEACE

Tranquility, calm, serenity. A state of harmony, quiet, an absence of crisis or chaos. Existence in a state of acceptance. The ability to live "life on life's terms" with some ease and comfort. The opposite of chaos or turmoil, of being uncomfortable, feeling in danger, or experiencing stress or anxiety.

PEER PRESSURE

Pressure or coercion to do something that is exerted by a person's equals, colleagues, cohorts. Although the pressure may not be actively exerted, it may be perceived to exist. Friends, family, siblings, schoolmates, and co-workers are examples of peers. Peer pressure is something individuals face from "people, places, and things" that may create obstacles to being clean or abstinent. Alternatively, peer pressure can be positive; a person in recovery who surrounds himself or herself with clean/sober/abstinent friends will feel positive peer pressure to stay in recovery.

PEOPLE, PLACES, AND THINGS

The persons, locations, and items associated with an individual's using, drinking, or participating in addictive behaviors; may include the physical location where drug use or addictive behavior occurred and/or the activities, paraphernalia, etc. that are associated with active addiction. Also referred to as "old playmates, playgrounds, and playthings."

PERCEPTION

Awareness, insight, discernment. The way a person looks at things. Past experiences, knowledge, feelings, judgments, attitudes, etc. that affect one's interpretation of a given situation. In recovery, it is important for an individual to check his or her perception of events against that of trusted friends or sponsors.

PERFECTION

Flawlessness, rightness, excellence. The state of being without blemishes, defects, or shortcomings. To arrive at a state at which one does not require any further work, recovery, transformation, or change. Recovery is a state of "progress, not perfection."

PERSEVERANCE

Resolve, continuous steady action and/or belief, often in spite of great difficulty. A spiritual principle that calls for remaining on the path of recovery through difficult, unfortunate, or painful times. Staying clean/sober/abstinent and continuing to work in recovery through tumultuous situations, illnesses, relationships ending, and the like.

PERSONAL INVENTORY

Also known as a "Fourth-Step Inventory," "Moral Inventory," and "Tenth Step Inventory." Part of the Fourth- and Tenth-Step processes.

When used in reference to the Tenth Step, taking personal inventory is the listing and writing about present-day assets, defects, fears, resentments etc., to discover the exact nature of current behavior patterns in recovery. There are many different formats available. It is suggested that this part of the program be done nightly, before retiring, as part of one's reflection on one's behavior and feelings that day, in order to enhance the maintenance of one's spiritual fitness.

PERSONALITY

Individuality, persona, character. The collection of physical expressions and character traits, including assets and defects, a person possesses, as well as the attitude he or she expresses toward life. The unique expression of one's nature and character in the way one may dress, speak, or carry him- or herself.

PERSPECTIVE

Perception, outlook, point of view. A particular view of a situation or a way of seeing things, whether in a positive or negative manner. May change if new information is gathered or if viewed in light of alternative considerations or from a transcended or enlightened point of view.

PITFALLS

Snare, downside, hazard. An unexpected danger, usually as the result of one's not being cognizant of one's surroundings or situation. Examples in recovery may include unhealthy relationships, living beyond one's means, and/or becoming too involved in service or some other aspect of the program and getting out of balance with the rest of the program.

PLAN(S)

Program, scheme, method. A set of ideas or suggestions as to a course of action. May be a set of goals or objectives or a path to achieve those goals or objectives. Setting an appointment or making a commitment to perform an activity with another person.

POLICY/POLICIES

Strategy, rules, guidelines. The guidelines by which the business of a fellowship is conducted. Used during business meetings, subcommittee meetings, etc. Policies are suggested and voted on by the group (group conscience). Often based on the collective experience of what has worked well in the past.

POTENTIAL

Probable, likely, possible. Also refers to the level to which someone or something could possibly rise, goals that one can achieve, or the abilities one has within him- or herself that are yet to be realized. One's potential is what he or she is capable of.

POWER

Energy, force, control. The ability to generate action, a source of strength, vigor, etc.

POWER GREATER THAN OURSELVES

A benevolent force outside of oneself that has more strength than one possesses. A "higher power" or power other than a person that can effect a restoration to sanity. A "power greater than ourselves" is first mentioned in Step Two of the Twelve Steps. The concept of a power greater than oneself is key to working a twelve-step program of recovery.

POWERLESS

Ineffective, immobilized, defenseless. The state of being without power, particularly regarding the disease of addiction. Having no control over a situation, being unable to control behavior or actions, e.g., unable to control the use of drugs, alcohol, behaviors, feelings, etc. Having no control over people, places, and things.

PRACTICAL APPLICATION

Actively putting to a special use. Putting a plan into action, applying what has been learned. Taking concrete and defined steps toward a stated goal to achieve a particular outcome, which may include being free from active addiction. In recovery, putting the steps into action in one's life is an example of practical application of the program.

PRACTICE

Carry out, perform, apply. Engage in an activity or task to increase one's proficiency at that activity or task or to prepare for an upcoming activity or task of increased difficulty. We "… practice these principles in all our affairs," says the Twelfth Step, which is a direction to persons in the fellowships to live the Twelve Steps in every aspect of their lives to the best of their abilities in order to enjoy long-lasting recovery.

PRAYER

Entreaty, appeal, plea. The act of communication with a higher power or God of one's understanding. May take many forms, formal or informal, with ritual or through simple communication in a conversational manner, in solitude or in communion with others, in any body posture, including on one's knees. This practice can change, evolve, and grow over time, as one's understanding of recovery changes and grows.

PREDECESSOR(S)

Forerunner, ancestor, precursor. One who came before. The first people or group to do something; pioneers. People involved in the beginning of a movement. The individuals who founded the twelve-step programs and created the model for today's recovery programs. The authors of recovery literature, service manuals, etc. who gave of themselves in order for the fellowships to survive and flourish.

PRESTIGE

Honor, regard, high esteem. Self-important concern about prestige can draw one's attention away from the primary purpose of a twelve-step program and prevent one from developing the humility needed for the surrender that is a part of the twelve-step recovery process.

In recovery, prestige is a by-product of living life according to twelve-step principles. Any prestige that attaches to one will be in the nature of admiration and friendship bestowed by peers and based on how one lives and applies program principles in all of one's affairs.

PRIDE

Arrogance, conceit, smugness. The opposite of humility. Can be a character defect when it sets one apart from others as being better than them. But pride can be a positive feeling of accomplishment, as in taking pride in one's work, actions, hygiene, etc. One avoids feeling too "proud" of one's recovery, as that often leads to delusions of self-sufficiency or self-reliance, which frequently lead to feelings of invulnerability, of not needing the program, and often, a relapse.

PRIMARY PURPOSE

The priority, the first task. In twelve-step programs, "to carry the message to the addict [alcoholic, etc.] who still suffers" is the primary purpose. The message is that recovery is possible; that the program, if followed, will lead to a life of recovery.

PRINCIPLES (SPIRITUAL PRINCIPLES)

Ethics, morality, values. Referring to spiritual principles found within the steps that form a code of conduct by which to live. Positive actions, sometimes called opposite actions, recovering people strive to live by that are found embedded in the Twelve Steps, Twelve Traditions, and Twelve Concepts. Some examples include: hope, faith, trust, patience, courage, perseverance, humility, honesty, willingness, open-mindedness, service, tolerance, compassion, and anonymity, which is described as the "spiritual foundation" of all the traditions.

PRIORITY

Right-of-way, precedence, main concern. Something requiring immediate attention. The present matter or the issue that must be addressed before other things. In recovery, the action or task that comes before all others, and upon which everything else depends, including, work, returning to or furthering one's education, relationships, children's demands, etc. Most twelve-step programs encourage its members to make their recovery a priority.

PRIVACY

Confidentiality, discretion, solitude. The keeping of possessions, thoughts, or valuables secure or private. Keeping intimate personal information secure. Privacy is not the same as isolation. It is appropriate for some conversations and activities to be carried on in privacy; however, in recovery one learns the difference between maintaining a healthy and respectful privacy and an unhealthy isolation. A sponsor keeps the sponsee's confidences; this builds trust and is about privacy; it is not the same as keeping secrets, which is negative and unhealthy.

Keeping one's anonymity in public is an example of healthy privacy.

PRIVILEGE

Advantage, license, benefit. Something not guaranteed or something one does not necessarily have a right to. A "perk" or benefit that comes as the result of performance or one's actions. Privileges must be earned by behavior; they may be granted or withheld based on one's actions.

PROCESS

Method, course of action, procedure. Continuing development requiring many changes; involving many components and variables. Refers to the idea that recovery does not happen overnight, instantly, or quickly. The position that a person in recovery will never be "fully" recovered and that recovery is an ongoing course of action or development. The process of recovery is said to take place in stages, first physically, then mentally/emotionally, and finally spiritually. Relapse is believed to occur in the opposite order; first spiritually, then emotionally/mentally, and then physically."

PROCRASTINATION

Delaying, postponing, deferring. Refers to an action that needs to be/should be taken. Avoiding action because of subconscious fear or because of laziness, time constraints, financial situations, character defects, etc. Delaying an action by conscious choice. Looking for alternatives to an unpleasant or undesirable task or allowing oneself to be distracted by miscellaneous and unnecessary tasks prior to finally doing what is required.

PROGESSION

Advance, development, evolution. Continuous forward movement. To continue on a particular track, be it negative or positive. In active addiction, progression may mean needing more of a particular drug to get high than was needed previously as more drugs may be required to reach the same level of impairment.

In recovery, the Twelve Steps follow a positive progression, each step building upon the last, as the person in recovery learns more skills to deal with situations the longer he or she stays clean or abstinent.

PROJECTION

Forecasting, prediction, envisioning. In recovery, often refers to worrying about situations or events that may not occur or fearing a specific outcome. May also refer to assuming one knows the thoughts of others, such as their disapproval, which may really be a "projection" of one's own feelings about oneself onto them.

Associated with thinking of negative outcomes or having expectations. Thinking the worst thing that could happen, will happen. A mindset that horrible things will occur.

PROMISE(S)

Vow, commitment, agreement. A guarantee of something to come when directions or suggestions are followed in a twelve-step program. The Big Book of Alcoholics Anonymous contains twelve statements that have come to be known as "The Promises," which outline what one can expect to achieve through working the Twelve Steps. In Narcotics Anonymous there is one promise, "freedom from active addiction," if an addict works the Twelve Steps.

PROMOTION

Endorsement, advertising, back-up. The practice of claiming superiority of a product or service, putting one method or system above others. In the Twelve Traditions, the value of promotion is contrasted with the value of attraction; the tradition asserts that recovery fellowships will not proselytize or attempt to gain members through advertising or promotion, but rather that the individual members' actions as program members in recovery should be the thing that attracts new members.

PROVEN

Verified, confirmed, established. Shown to be true. A fact or statement that has been demonstrated with examples, such as people in twelve-step fellowships have the ability to find recovery from addiction through the Twelve Steps.

PRUDENCE

Carefulness, caution, discretion. Good sense, forethought. Responsible behavior, doing what is necessary or warranted, without making rash or frivolous decisions.

A group or service body in a twelve-step program is charged with being prudent, or responsible, with fellowship money. An individual using discretion with resources, money, or actions is showing prudence.

PUBLIC INFORMATION/PUBLIC RELATIONS

Image management, publicity, marketing. The process of making others aware of an organization by various available media, including flyers, mailers, presentations, advertisements, television, radio, movies, and the Internet; offering information about the primary purpose of an organization, where meetings may be found, etc. The Twelve Traditions advise that recovery fellowships should engage in a public relations policy of "attraction rather than promotion."

PURPOSE

Intention, function, rationale. A reason for doing something. The primary purpose is the first purpose; the primary purpose of twelve-step fellowships is for each member to stay clean/sober/abstinent and to help others who wish to recover to do so.

RAGE

Temper, wrath, fury. Intense anger, often manifesting itself in violence. A very serious and intense expression of the feeling of anger, which, if not addressed or treated, can be damaging to the recovery process and to relationships. Anger is a normal human emotion, but if it gets out of control or out of balance, it can become rage. Acting on rage is usually indicative of more serious issues.

RATIONALIZE

Justify, diminish, explain. To attempt to make one's behavior or past actions seem reasonable. Trying to make unacceptable behavior appear acceptable.

RCM (REGIONAL COMMITTEE MEMBER)

A program member elected to represent his or her area on the Regional Service Committee (RSC). An area may have two regional committee members. An RCM carries the area conscience on motions on which votes have been cast, learns about upcoming events, and is the link between the area service committee and the regional service committee.

RD (REGIONAL DELEGATE)

A member elected by the Regional Service Committee to carry the regional conscience to the World Service Conference. The RD is the link between the regional service conference and the World Service Conference and traditionally is responsible for conducting service workshops and/or conference agenda workshops.

READY

Prepared, equipped, organized. The Sixth Step says one must be "entirely ready" to ask a higher power to remove his or her character defects—this means to have no reservations, doubts, or hesitation. To be in a state of willingness and preparedness.

REALITY

Truth, actuality, existence. That which actually could or does exist, as opposed to an imaginary or false nature. The state of being from which drugs and alcohol often provided an escape. In recovery, one embraces reality or "life on life's terms"; one does not attempt to escape from it.

REBELLIOUSNESS

Defiance, obstinacy, noncompliance. Rebellion is often the act of doing something simply because it is the opposite of what another person or group wishes one to do.

RECIPROCAL

Joint, shared, mutual. Characterized by give-and-take. The action of returning what was given in kind or providing another thing in return that is of equal or greater value. A sponsorship relationship, friendship, or any relationship wherein two people give to one another equally or nearly so.

RECOVERY

Revival, healing, revitalization. A return to a former state of usefulness or health. In recovery, the process of building a new, drug-free life out of the desperation of active addiction. The process of getting and staying clean/sober/abstinent.

"Recovery" has a meaning far beyond the idea of mere abstinence, and it includes the process of correcting behaviors or learning new and healthier patterns for one's life through working and living the Twelve Steps. Recovery is a lifelong process with many different mechanisms, systems, or components, but predominately involving the Twelve Steps. To live a life in recovery is to live in freedom from the slavery of addiction and in a full, rich, and rewarding way that has meaning and value.

REGRET

Remorse, grief, repentance. A feeling of sorrow, shame, or guilt about one's past behaviors or events that took place in the past. Having a guilty conscience or feeling shame because of the damage one has caused or the wreckage one has created. To feel unhappy about missing an opportunity or not taking positive advantage of a situation when it presented itself. To feel responsible for the things done when one was in active addiction.

RELAPSE

Setback, deterioration, decline. To "go back to." The state of returning to an old pattern of behavior, whether it is using drugs or some other negative, maladaptive behavior. Not a necessary part of recovery, but it does occur. Relapse is a process that begins when a person stops taking the necessary actions to maintain recovery (such as going to meetings and working the Twelve Steps) and culminates in the actual use of mind- and/or mood-altering chemicals or the return to a destructive behavior.

RELATED FACILITIES AND OUTSIDE ENTERPRISES

This phrase is an excerpt from the Twelve Traditions; it usually refers to treatment centers and/or hospitals that treat individuals with addiction, but may be clubhouses or other structures.

RELATIONSHIP(S)

Association, liaison, bond. A relationship is a connection between ideas, things, or people. Types include intimate, sexual, family, marital, romantic, sponsorship, acquaintance, etc. Establishing and maintaining communication with another individual or group and having shared experiences with each other are generally considered important parts of relationships.

RELAX

Unwind, slow down, loosen up. To take time out from one's schedule for rest and/or recreation. Lowering one's heart rate, blood pressure, level of anxiety, or preoccupation with current events through prayer, meditation, or spending time reading, resting, listening to music, journaling, watching television, exercising, or praying.

RELIGION

Creed, faith, belief. The organized study of the divine or spiritual aspect of life. Compliance with a way of life that its advocates believe puts them into a relationship with the divine.

A group or organization devoted to a particular belief system and usually with a single leader, responsible for the group, who is in the position to give directives to the members.

A group of people who worship the same idea of a deity in a certain traditional manner.

REMORSE

Repentance, shame, regret. The feeling of responsibility, sadness, or sorrow for past actions. Not to be wallowed-in; however, it is possible that being aware of one's remorse can have a positive effect if it motivates a person to change his or her behavior.

REPARATION(S)

Compensation, reimbursement, damages. The action of making amends by taking responsibility for one's actions. May include approaching the person one has harmed, taking responsibility for the incident or situation, and offering to repair the situation in either a financial manner or through action. This includes rectifying a situation when possible and making every effort to live in such a way as will not cause damage or harm in the future.

REPRESSION

Subjugation, oppression. "Squashing," pushing down, or suppressing feelings or knowledge about unpleasant or painful realities. Victims of abuse or extreme stress may use repression to suppress painful memories; persons in recovery may repress true knowledge of harms they have done.

REPRIEVE

Pardon, acquittal, amnesty. To give temporary relief or delay from punishment or pain. In recovery, it is believed one achieves only a reprieve from active addiction, not a permanent cure. The length and quality of the reprieve depends upon the degree of one's practice of the Twelve Steps.

RESCUE

Save, set free, release. To assist a person to safety or free him or her from danger. In recovery, may be the well-intentioned action of interfering with another person's recovery by preventing him or her from facing the consequences of his or her actions.

RESENTMENT

Bitterness, dislike, ill feelings for a person, place, or institution with whom one has come into conflict. Often these feelings will linger long after the initial problem is resolved. Resentment causes a person to relive a situation repeatedly, instead of attempting to let go or surrender. Even when a person has a legitimate grievance, to hang on to old resentments only damages his or her recovery.

RESERVATION

Stipulation, reluctance, unwillingness. A loophole left in a recovery program that may lead to a relapse. Considered insidious and often hidden; a person may not realize he or she has any. Examples include: "If my mother, father, child, spouse, etc. dies, I don't know if I can stay clean," or "If I find out I have a deadly disease, I am going to use drugs."

RESISTANCE

Opposition, refusal, defiance. A negative reaction to trying anything new, such as recovery. The opposite of open-mindedness and willingness, two qualities necessary for recovery.

RESPECT

Esteem, reverence, high regard. A spiritual principle, it includes admiration or deference toward a person or group.

RESOURCES

Source, assets, wealth. Something that can offer assistance, such as a sponsor, recovery literature, meeting attendance, reaching out, the fellowship, a peer or support group, friends with more time in recovery than one has, service commitments, etc. Anything that an individual can access to assist with the process of recovery.

RESPONSIBILITY

Accountability, dependability, conscientiousness. Being able to be relied upon. Doing the work necessary to provide for one's needs. Not relying or depending on another to do work that one can/should do for him- or herself. Making decisions and thinking about how the consequences may affect others.

RESTORATION

Return, restitution, re-establishment. The process of returning something to a previous or former state of health, perfection, or wholeness. The Second Step states that a higher power can "restore" a recovering person's sanity, indicating that he or she once enjoyed the state of mental health and can again through the twelve-step process.

RESULTS

Consequences, outcomes, effects. The evidence of work completed. What a recovering person gets out of working the Twelve Steps that is directly proportionate to the effort he or she puts into the recovery program. Results may be clean time, social acceptability, healthy relationships, or spiritual, emotional, mental, and physical balance.

REVEAL

Disclose, tell, make public. To make something visible or uncover something. By continuing to work the program in all aspects of one's life, "more will be revealed," about oneself, one's relationship with one's higher power, and one's relationships with others.

RISK

Jeopardy, danger, threat. Also refers to the act of taking the chance of losing one thing in order to gain another; maybe losing a negative quality or virtue in order to gain a positive asset. Venturing out of one's comfort zone in order to grow, learn something new, etc.

RIGHTEOUSNESS

Virtue, morality, decency. The character trait of doing the right things for the right reasons; behaving in a just or upright manner with integrity and self-respect. Behaving properly can be a result of working a recovery program and learning how to live right. However, self-righteousness is a character defect often used to prop up one's own ego and make others feel small.

RIGOROUS

Exact, thorough, meticulous. A continuous and regular effort in a particular area; building strength and stamina. Steady effort put into a program of recovery; creating results based on the Twelve Steps that foster great growth.

SANITY

Mental health, good sense, wisdom. The ability to deal with reality as it is. The state of being sane or having a sound mind; results in healthy decision-making based on knowledge of real-life experience and consequences rather than on fantasy or wishful thinking.

SEARCHING

Penetrating, probing, incisive. Referring to a "searching and fearless moral inventory," an in-depth and honest evaluation of the ways addiction affected every area of one's life, including acknowledgement of addiction's effects on the lives of others. A searching inventory leaves nothing out and digs deeper than surface level circumstances to discover the root of the problem, issue, or behavior. To discover the motives, desires, and expectations that underlie one's behaviors.

SECOND STEP

From the Twelve Steps (Step Two), it states that a person begins to believe that his or her sanity can be restored by a higher power.

SECOND TRADITION

From the Twelve Traditions (Tradition Two), it states that for purposes of the twelve-step group there are no leaders, but that there is one "ultimate authority, a loving God as he may express himself in the group conscience." Leaders are described as "trusted servants . . . (who) do not govern."

SECRET(S)

Clandestine, undisclosed, hidden. Information a person keeps to him- or herself, either personal or about another person or situation. A secret is not shared with another person and might concern past or present behavior or actions one feels shame about. A secret may constitute a reservation in one's program that can contribute to relapse. Undisclosed information about a person that will keep that person sick, prone to relapse, or unable to change behavior in a certain area.

SECURITY

Safety, well-being, sanctuary. Can also mean a guarantee. A feeling of security is needed in order to feel free and able to communicate or express one's feelings in the confidence that one's privacy will be respected.

SELF

Identity, personality, person. Of and pertaining to needs or wants of the individual person, sometimes to the exclusion of others. Selfishness and self-centeredness have long been considered among the defining character defects of those with addiction.

SELF-ABSORPTION

Completely concerned with self. To think only and mostly of self. When a situation arises the first thought is "how will this affect me?" with little or no regard to the effect the situation will have on others. A character defect.

SELF-CENTERED

Egotistical; believing oneself to be the center of any situation, whether in a negative or a positive way (either "everybody hates me" or "everybody loves me"). Evaluating everything and everyone in terms of their relation and usefulness to the self. Similar to self-obsessed. A character defect.

SELF-DECEPTION (SELF-DELUSION)

Lies "told" to the self. A refusal to accept the truth, usually about one's role in past or present wrongdoings. A refusal to acknowledge the reality of a situation or of one's behaviors. The attempt to manage and control one's addiction by making claims that one can stop at any time or that the behavior is not as bad as it actually is are examples of self-deception.

SELF-ESTEEM

Self-worth, confidence, self-respect. The value one places on oneself. Depending on one's opinion of oneself, self-esteem is often characterized as "good" or "bad," "high" or "low." In recovery, self-esteem is boosted by performing service, step work, etc.

SELF-OBSESSION

Incessant thoughts of self, fixated on self. An inability to think of anything other than one's own needs and desires, often at the expense of others, and with little or no regard to how one's actions may affect them.

SELF-PITY

The belief that one's own life is harder or sadder than that of anyone else. This feeling is usually accompanied by a lack of gratitude and makes it difficult to remember that in each life there are both negative and positive elements.

SELF-RESPECT

Pride; dignity, confidence. A spiritual principle; the act of honoring one's self in manner, behavior, or interaction with others. A habit of reverence for self and for acting with integrity and with regard for the effect one's actions will have on the self and others.

SELF-RIGHTEOUS(NESS)

The belief that one is always correct or that one knows more than others. The inability to admit when one is wrong. Often accompanied by attempts to defend one's own actions or point of view at all costs or at the expense of others. May be the result of fear, and is often a way to deflect criticism or make others out to be insignificant.

SELF-SEEKING

Egocentric, egotistical, vain. Always looking for ways to attract attention or to improve one's own position. This characteristic may cause one to try to become a "big shot" or "guru" in his or her fellowship, boasting of the number of sponsees he or she has, the speed with which he or she did the steps, etc.

SELF-SUFFICIENT (SELF-SUFFICIENCY)

Self-reliant, self-contained, independent. A character defect when it prevents someone in recovery from establishing a relationship with or accepting help from his or her higher power or others in recovery. May cover a lack of trust or faith.

SELF-SUPPORTING

Self-financing, self-sustaining, successful. All twelve-step fellowships follow the Seventh Tradition injunction to be "self-supporting through our own contributions." This is to avoid the problems of outside influence (interference) that accepting donations from those outside the fellowships would inevitably involve.

SELF-WILL

Determination to have one's own way with no consideration of others' wishes, desires, rights, or feelings. To act on impulse and disregard principles. An addictive behavior in which one ignores the principles of recovery or does not attempt to take into consideration the will of one's higher power.

SELF-WORTH

The value one places on him- or herself. Generally, one's self-worth is low after a period of active addiction. Living in recovery almost always results in an elevated sense of self-worth.

SELFISH

Egotistical, greedy, insatiable. Believing or acting as if one's wants or needs are of greater importance than the wants or needs of another. Thinking only of oneself and putting the rights, wants, needs, desires of others second. Considered a character defect.

SENSITIVE

Perceptive, susceptible, receptive. Easily hurt or upset; touchy. Inversely, can mean alert, finely tuned, responsive.

People in active addiction often demonstrate extreme sensitivity to slights (real or perceived) against themselves, but not so much to the feelings of others. The twelve-step process enables people in recovery to turn that sensitivity outward, and instead of focusing on his or her own hurt feelings, respond to the hurts felt by others and try to help them.

SERENITY

Peacefulness, tranquility, contentment. A sense of calm during crisis, stress, complications and upsets. Serenity is the hallmark of recovery—rather than feeling the old edginess, restlessness, and impatience of addictive needs that can never really be satisfied.

Serenity means feeling grounded and connected to one's higher power and to the people who surround one; feeling connected to one's life, and being emotionally, mentally, physically, and spiritually balanced. Serenity can be achieved through prayer and meditation and when practicing the Twelve Steps.

SERVICE

Help, assistance, benefit. Helping other people, groups, or institutions; usually associated with volunteering one's time and committing a certain portion of that time either once or on a regular basis. In meetings, service may consist of setting up, cleaning up, sharing when called upon, making coffee, acting as secretary, treasurer, etc. Sponsorship or area-, regional-, or world-level commitments are forms of service, as is contributing during the Seventh-Tradition collection.

SERVICE BOARDS

As defined in the Twelve Traditions, service boards consist of members elected by a service committee to oversee an office or corporate entity, such as a district or central office of a twelve-step fellowship.

SERVICE CENTERS

A physical structure/building that is usually a literature distribution center, meeting facility for service boards, information clearinghouse, and more. Funded through a combination of member, area, and regional donations, as well as by literature sales. Service centers may employ program members to do jobs that would ordinarily have to be done by non-members, which is not the same as paying a recovering person for service work. Service work is done as a part of working the Twelfth Step and is strictly unpaid.

SEVENTH STEP

From the Twelve Steps (Step Seven); it requires one to humbly ask his or her higher power to remove his or her shortcomings (character defects). Step Seven uses the word "humbly," which indicates that humility is the key to this step. Humility is distinctly different from humiliation; it is a realistic acceptance of one's own humanity; one's assets as well as deficiencies, and involves the knowledge that help is needed in order to continue on the path of recovery.

SEVENTH TRADITION

From the Twelve Traditions (Tradition Seven); it states that each twelve-step group should support itself financially and not accept funding or donations from outside organizations or non-members. This is to avoid the problems of outside influence (interference) that accepting donations from those outside the fellowships would inevitably involve, discussed in the definition on self-sufficiency. Being self-supporting is also a way of being responsible for oneself at the group level.

SEX AND LOVE ADDICTS ANONYMOUS (SLAA)

A twelve-step fellowship of men and women whose primary focus is to help each with sex and love addiction. Members believe that this may take several different forms including, but not limited to, a compulsive need for sex, extreme dependency on one or many people, or a chronic preoccupation with romance, intrigue, or fantasy. Its recovery text is called *Sex and Love Addicts Anonymous*. There are SLAA meetings in twenty-five countries including the US.

SHAME

Disgrace, dishonor, humiliation. A painful feeling many persons continue to carry into recovery. Shame involves regret or embarrassment because of immoral, dangerous, or illegal past activities either engaged in to obtain and use substances or act on addictive behavior, or due to the lack of inhibition produced by active addiction. Shame can be relieved during thorough Fourth and Fifth Steps, as well as after Ninth Step amends are made.

SHARE (SHARING)

Impart, reveal, disclose. Speaking up when called on in a twelve-step meeting for the purpose of letting members of the group know more about the speaker's "experience, strength, and hope." This allows newcomers in the group to learn how the program works and what it has done for others, familiarizes newcomers with potential sponsors, and contributes to the feeling of fellowship within the group. Each group and meeting has different guidelines and etiquette for sharing.

SHORTCOMINGS

Inadequacies, failings, faults. Related to the character defects that were revealed in the Fourth and Fifth Steps, and which the Seventh Step seeks to have one's higher power remove.

SIGNIFICANT OTHER

Life partner, mate, companion. May be a spouse or live-in lover. Not reflective of any specific sexual orientation or lifestyle.

SIMPLICITY

Straightforward, uncomplicated, unfussiness. Desirable in recovery, reflected in expressions like "keep it simple." Twelve-step fellowships often refer to themselves as "simple programs for complicated people."

SIXTH STEP

From the Twelve Steps (Step Six), in which the recovering person declares him- or herself completely willing to have his or her character defects removed.

SIXTH TRADITION

From the Twelve Traditions (Tradition Six); which states that twelve-step groups should never endorse any related businesses or institutions in case the usual problems, such as ownership, status, or finance, divert the group from its original goal of helping persons seeking recovery.

SNIPER SHARING

Contradicting or belittling a previous speaker while sharing at a twelve-step meeting. When sharing, it is customary to share one's "experience, strength and hope." Opinions do vary and a person may disagree with what someone else has shared in a respectful manner without "sniping," or making obvious or pointed remarks or insults.

If a member has a problem with another member's sharing, it should be discussed person-to-person, respectfully, after the meeting.

SOBRIETY

Abstinence, clear-headedness, thoughtfulness. Terminology used primarily in the fellowship of Alcoholics Anonymous. The state of being free from the drug alcohol. Describes one recovering from the disease of alcoholism.

"Sobriety" is considered in a similar vein as "recovery," as a state of being that is very desirable, positive, and enriching, a way of life that includes adherence to twelve-step principles, and that is much more than mere "abstinence" or "being dry."

SOCIALLY ACCEPTABLE/SOCIAL ACCEPTABILITY

Unstigmatized, not demonized. Something regarded as tolerable and respectable by the public. Relating to the manner in which people in groups behave and interact with one another, "socially acceptable" refers to what is considered "good" behavior, cooperation, kindness, etc.

Something that is socially acceptable is considered either a benign or a positive influence on the community, causing no harm to others.

SOLUTION(S)

Answer, explanation, way out. The key to a puzzle or the answer to a problem. In recovery, the Twelve Steps are pointed out as a solution to the disease of addiction.

SPECIAL WORKERS

Employees, whether in recovery or not, who are paid for their work for the twelve-step programs/fellowships. Special workers are not volunteers in their chosen fellowship.

SPECIAL INTEREST MEETING

A meeting classification commonly called "common needs" meetings. A recovery meeting for people of a particular group. The primary purpose of these meetings is always to carry the message of recovery to the addict who still suffers. No person in recovery will be turned away even if they do not belong to the common need or special interest group (a referral may be made to a general interest group after the meeting). Examples of special interest meetings may include meetings for young people, gay and lesbian (GLBT), women only, men only, professionals (e.g., doctors, lawyers, entertainers,) etc. for whom anonymity may be especially important or difficult to achieve in an ordinary open or closed twelve-step meeting.

SPIRIT

Courage, strength, force. The unseen quality within a human being that is not physical; that which motivates an individual to evolve or connect to a higher power or from which the feelings of an individual stem. That part of the being connected to a higher consciousness. Sometimes called soul, essence, inner self, life-force, chi.

SPIRITUAL

Sacred, holy, devout. Of or pertaining to the non-material, non-physical. The belief in a higher power, higher consciousness, or universal truths; not necessarily a "God" associated with religion. Having to do with principles that are timeless and universal instead of immediate and particular. Having a focus on a collective well-being as opposed to only being concerned with the self.

SPIRITUAL AWAKENING

An awareness of a spiritual nature. Having insight into one's life that was previously unavailable. Transcending a current situation and viewing that situation with a different opinion, feeling, or perception. The realization that one has the ability to live by principles.

The Twelfth Step says that once one has had a spiritual awakening as the result of working the steps, the next action is to carry the message to those who still suffer [from addiction] who wish to recover.

SPIRITUAL PRINCIPLES (PRINCIPLES)

Philosophy, values, beliefs. Referring to spiritual principles found within the steps, these are a suggested code of conduct by which to live. Positive actions, sometimes called "opposite actions," that recovering people strive to live by and are found embedded in the Twelve Steps, Traditions, and Concepts. Examples include: hope, faith, trust, patience, courage, perseverance, humility, honesty, willingness, open-mindedness, service, anonymity, tolerance, compassion, etc.

SPIRITUALITY

Belief in or practice of transcending the human experience of survival and carnal needs in pursuit of something higher, be it a higher consciousness or higher power. The pursuit of connection with a universal truth or consciousness. The act of striving for transcendence of a current situation in pursuit of a higher, deeper, wiser understanding and/or connectedness.

SPONSEE

An individual who is being sponsored and guided through the Twelve Steps by another individual in recovery.

SPONSOR

Backer, supporter, liaison. A person who guides another person (usually a newcomer) through working the Twelve Steps. A sponsor need not have any particular length of recovery, but it is generally thought that he or she should have a sponsor of his or her own, should have worked the Twelve Steps him- or herself, and participate in his or her chosen fellowship. It is suggested that every recovering person acquire and use the assistance of a sponsor when working the Twelve Steps.

SPONSORSHIP

The relationship between two recovering people wherein one serves as a mentor, teacher, or guide through the Twelve Steps of the program. The act of sponsoring another person. Sponsors each have their own ways of working with their sponsees. There is no one way to sponsor.

SPONSORSHIP FAMILY

A group of recovering persons connected through sponsorship. A "grand-sponsor" is the person who sponsors the sponsor; "great grand-sponsor" sponsors the grand-sponsor; "sponsee brothers" or "sponsee sisters" share the same sponsor. (These are not official titles, simply affectionate terms that have become accepted through usage.) These people may also become part of the recovering person's support group. Some coordinate gatherings, weekend events, or private meetings to celebrate their recovery together as "families.".

STAYING CLEAN

Remaining spotless, fresh, unspoiled. To continue to be abstinent from all mind- and mood-altering chemicals and activities with the purpose of recovering from addiction. Substances and activities may include prescription or street drugs, alcohol, compulsive gambling, sex, shopping, video-gaming, etc.

STEPS (TWELVE STEPS)

The Twelve Steps are the basis of all recovery programs referred to as "Twelve Step Programs." Originally developed by the founders of Alcoholics Anonymous and based on the "Four Absolutes" of the Oxford Group (an early Christian-based group with an interest in helping alcoholics, or drunkards, as they were then called). Because they work when one works them, the Twelve Steps have become the "gold standard" for treating addiction, from overeating to pornography.

The Twelve Steps are performed in a specific order because each one lays the foundation for the next. This sequential process assists a person in recovering from addiction. The steps are best done under a sponsor's guidance.

STEP EIGHT

From the Twelve Steps (Eighth Step), it requires the addict to make a list of the people he or she has harmed and become willing to make amends to them all. The Fourth Step inventory is usually used as a resource to help develop this list, as, paradoxically, often it is the people one has harmed whom one resents, and their names are typically on the Fourth Step list of wrongdoings and resentments.

STEP ELEVEN

From the Twelve Steps (Eleventh Step), it calls for continued prayer and meditation to improve conscious contact with one's higher power. According to the step, one's prayer should only be to gain knowledge of that power's will for one and the ability to carry it out.

STEP FIVE

From the Twelve Steps (Fifth Step), it calls for addicts to admit to their higher power, another person, and to themselves the exact nature of their wrongs. The step during which an addict relates the inventory created during the Fourth Step to his or her sponsor and discusses the findings thereof with focus on removing the defects the inventory has outlined.

STEP FOUR

From the Twelve Steps (Step Four). Calls for a "searching and fearless" moral inventory. The particulars of working this step may vary according to fellowship attended. For example, some fellowships have people write a narrative/story or make a list or write in columns, but whatever format is followed, the Fourth Step inventory is a written assessment by a person in recovery of his or her own past deeds, revealing resentments, strengths and weaknesses, character defects, all aspects of his or her relationships, as well as assets. The point is to "inventory" one's character and to get rid of what is damaged and to see what needs to built up for continued healthy growth.

The Fourth Step is often approached with great fear by the newcomer, but there is no need for this. All the millions of people, all over the world, who have achieved lasting, long-term recovery through twelve-step programs, have taken Fourth Steps. While writing down one's past deeds might be embarrassing or even emotionally upsetting, it is never going to be as bad as having done those deeds in the first place! An understanding sponsor will be of great help in taking this step.

Old timers who have gone through the steps, including the Fourth Step, numerous times, insist that the Fourth Step is where true relief from the suffering of addiction begins.

STEP NINE

From the Twelve Steps (Ninth Step), it calls for the recovering person to make amends to all people he or she has harmed (listed in Step Eight), except when doing so would injure either the injured party or others.

STEP ONE

From the Twelve Steps (First Step), it requires acknowledgement of powerlessness over one's addiction, coupled with an admission that one's life has become unmanageable. The only step that must be done to perfection; as it logically calls for abstinence, which is the prerequisite for recovery. The admission of powerlessness paves the way for a realistic opinion of the self and lays the foundation of all the other steps.

STEP SEVEN

From the Twelve Steps (Seventh Step), it requires that the recovering person asks his or her higher power to remove his or her shortcomings in a spirit of humility. This may be done through formal prayer, or though a simple, conversational request to the God of one's own understanding.

STEP SIX

From the Twelve Steps (Sixth Step), it states that the recovering person has become entirely willing to have his or her higher power remove his or her character defects.

STEP TEN

From the Twelve Steps (Tenth Step), it requires ongoing personal inventories and continued admission of any wrongdoing, as soon as possible after it is committed.

STEP THREE

From the Twelve Steps (Third Step), it requires that the recovering person make a decision to turn his or her will over to a higher power as that person understands that power.

STEP TWELVE

From the Twelve Steps (Twelfth Step), it states that completion of the steps having resulted in a spiritual awakening, the person in recovery must now try to carry the message of recovery to other people suffering from addiction and practice the spiritual principles in all of his or her affairs.

STEP TWO

From the Twelve Steps (Second Step), it declares that a person has come to believe that a power greater than him- or herself could restore him or her to sanity.

STEP ZERO

Learning to do the daily basics of life prior to working a First Step in recovery; consists of things like getting regular rest, making one's bed, eating three square meals a day, attending to personal hygiene and health, daily meeting attendance, learning to pray, doing laundry, learning to make phone calls to friends in recovery, reading recovery literature, etc.

These things were typically neglected in active addiction, so relearning them or learning to do them for the first time, lays the groundwork for doing the Twelve Steps and participating in the recovery fellowship of one's choice.

STRENGTH
Potency, vigor, might. The power or perseverance necessary to complete a task or deal with a situation or an issue.

SUBSTITUTION
Replacing one object, thing, or behavior with another. The act of putting down one behavior or substance to pick up another or allowing the disease of addiction to manifest itself in different ways.

SUCCESS
Victory, triumph, achievement. An accomplishment. Success for a person in recovery might not consist of material success, but may simply be living serenely without picking up, relapsing, or acting out one day at a time.

SUGGESTIONS
Proposals, propositions, ideas. Recommendations based on the successes and failures of others who have attempted the same task and learned what works and what does not work. Not carrying the weight of commands or laws, suggestions may simply be concepts that have been successful for other members of recovery in collective experience.

SUICIDE
Deliberate self-killing; intentional, self-inflicted death. Suicide occurs in every culture, all over the world, in every age group and social class. Addiction increases the risk of deliberate suicide, as well as the risk of accidental suicide by overdose.

SUPPORT

To prop up, sustain, brace. To offer assistance to someone. Listening to someone who needs to talk, picking someone up for a meeting, or staying after a meeting to help someone are all examples of support in recovery.

SUPPORT GROUP

A group of clean/sober/abstinent people who assist one another in the recovery process. A support group may engage in sports, service, or social activities together. Central to this group will usually be a sponsor, sponsorship-family members, and those with whom one regularly attends meetings.

SURRENDER

Submit, yield, capitulate. To lay down arms, stop fighting, concede. Recovery begins with surrender, an admission, and can be conscious or not that whatever the individual was clinging to must be abandoned, whether it was alcohol, drugs, or a behavior. Once that initial surrender or "giving up" takes place, others follow, until the person realizes that "giving up" or surrendering to the will of the higher power, is in fact the way to "win" a new and healthy life

SURVIVE

Endure, live on, continue to exist. Also to last longer than, or live through, especially relating to a challenge or crisis.

SYMPTOMS

Signs, indications, warnings. Evidence of an illness. Symptoms of the disease of addiction go beyond the substance or behavior to which one is addicted. Examples of some of these symptoms are: selfishness and self-centeredness; hypersensitivity to criticism (real or perceived); being judgmental; being hypercritical (of self or others); dishonesty; being manipulative; isolationism; promiscuity, resentfulness, etc.

TAPES

Recordings, messages; from the technology of audio- or videotape, the recorded sounds or images of words or scenes. Used to refer to the succession of thoughts or ideas that stream through a person's mind when he or she contemplates addictive or other negative, damaging behaviors. "Playing the tape out," is another way of saying "thinking an idea through to the end," noting all the possible consequences and ramifications.

"Playing old tapes" may also refer to listening to old (mental) messages that tell one that he or she will never succeed in recovery, is "too old, too fat, too stupid, etc." to become a person in recovery. Listening to these old, negative messages may lead one to relapse.

TEACHABLE

Having the ability to listen to and benefit from lessons, examples, advice. To remain willing to learn and have an open mind. To know that there is always more to learn. To be open to continuing growth. An important quality in recovery.

TEMPTATION

Attraction, inducement, lure. A situation or "trigger" that creates an overwhelming idea or thought of using drugs. Anything that produces an extreme desire to use drugs or act on an addiction.

TENTH STEP

From the Twelve Steps (Step Ten), it calls for continuing to take a personal inventory and when wrong, promptly admitting it.

TENTH TRADITION

From the Twelve Traditions (Tradition Ten), it states that twelve-step programs have no opinion on outside issues so that the program's name is never drawn into public controversy.

THANKFUL

Gratified, appreciative, pleased. The state of being grateful for what one has, is given, or what one has always had, but never before appreciated. A necessary state for ongoing recovery and a spiritual principle.

THERAPEUTIC

Restorative, healing, beneficial. Leading to health. Can refer to behavior, or the attempt to treat or cure a disease, illness, or injury.

THIRD STEP

From the Twelve Steps (Step Three), it requires making a decision to turn one's will over to a higher power as one understands that power.

THIRD-STEP PRAYER

A prayer many addicts and alcoholics say, privately, throughout the day, or aloud and in unison at meetings. The exact wording of the prayer varies depending on the twelve-step program, but comes from the Third Step of those programs and involves asking a higher power to guide one's will and life, and guide one in his or her recovery; thereby showing one how to live by the principles of the program.

THIRD TRADITION

From the Twelve Traditions (Tradition Three); a guiding principle stating that the only requirement for membership in a twelve-step program is the desire to stop using, drinking, or acting on an addictive behavior. As long as one has this desire, no one else, in or out of the fellowship, can deny one membership or meeting attendance.

THIRTEENTH-STEPPING/THE THIRTEENTH STEP

A somewhat glib euphemism for what occurs when a member with a greater amount of time in recovery dates (or attempts to date) someone with less time in recovery, i.e., a newcomer. Considered predatory and dangerous, especially to the newcomer, who needs time and space to get his or her bearings, come to grips with newly uncovered emotions, and is usually in great pain and need. Given this volatile mix of conditions, a newcomer is often "ripe for the picking" by those who should know better. Known Thirteenth-Steppers are not accorded respect in twelve-step programs. Thirteenth-stepping in recovery fellowships can be compared to sexual harassment in the workplace.

THOROUGH

Methodical, painstaking, meticulous. To be complete, searching, and leave nothing undisclosed. To follow through to completion. The Fourth Step calls for a thorough moral inventory, leaving nothing out.

TOLERANCE

Broadmindedness, open-mindedness, acceptance of the differing views of other people. A spiritual principle of recovery that guides relations with others. "Live and let live" is an expression of tolerance. Neither tolerance nor acceptance should be confused with approval.

TOOLS

Apparatus, utensils, gear. In recovery, "tools" refer to the actions, prior experiences, or spiritual principles that can assist a recovering person to get and stay drug free. Examples include: having and using a sponsor, belonging to and phoning a support group, attending twelve-step meetings, reading recovery literature, having and keeping a service commitment, journaling, and working the Twelve Steps. Tools may be acquired from listening and sharing in meetings about what has worked for other recovering people and from active participation in the program.

TRADITIONS (TWELVE TRADITIONS)

Twelve guiding principles for the twelve-step groups that help to make sure the program continues and thrives. Originally written soon after the establishment of Alcoholics Anonymous, and adapted by other twelve-step programs, the Twelve Traditions apply to the fellowship in the same way the steps apply to the individual in recovery. They provide a structure, and outline the way in which the groups should relate to their members, the members to the groups, and the way the fellowship itself should relate to the world at large.

TRIGGERS

Prompts, instigators, stimuli. Sense memories, situations, or people from an individual's past that begin the thought process of using or engaging in maladaptive behaviors. Anything that provokes the desire to use. Examples include: music, smells, seeing certain people, having cash in one's pocket or wallet, getting angry, getting too happy, payday, etc.

TRUST

Confidence, reliance, certainty. A spiritual principle, important in recovery, and key to developing a relationship with a higher power. Trust is necessary between sponsor and sponsee and often develops between the addict and the group.

TRUSTWORTHY

Dependable, reliable, honest. A spiritual principle. A trustworthy person may be relied upon to keep promises and live up to responsibilities. A person in recovery learns that the way to gain others' trust is by being trustworthy.

TWELFTH STEP

From the Twelve Steps (Step Twelve), it states that once one has had a spiritual awakening as a result of working the first eleven steps, that person must carry the message of recovery to other people suffering from addiction and to practice the spiritual principles of the program in all of his or her affairs.

TWELFTH TRADITION

From the Twelve Traditions (Tradition Twelve), it states that anonymity is the foundation of all of the Twelve Traditions and advises placing "principles before personalities." The emphasis on principles rather than on individual personalities is intended to foster true humility based on an understanding that all are equal in the twelve-step fellowship, that there are no "big shots," and that the only true authority comes from one's higher power.

ULTIMATE AUTHORITY

The final, definitive, greatest, or supreme power, one without equal. In twelve-step recovery, refers to the higher power, which many equate with the idea of God. In the Twelve Traditions, reference to the "ultimate authority" is framed by the idea that twelve-step fellowships have no elected or appointed leaders who "manage" or "direct" others; rather there is one "ultimate authority," a "loving God" as expressed in the "group conscience" of fellowship members.

UNCONDITIONAL LOVE

Affection and positive regard given freely, without boundaries, requirements, or reservations. A spiritual principle. Loving someone "no matter what." Does *not* mean tolerating any unacceptable behavior, it means that love will never be withdrawn on the basis of some action by the loved one.

UNDERSTANDING

Sympathy, comprehension, insight. A spiritual principle. Understanding others helps one be patient, tolerant, and accepting with them.

UNIFORMITY

Sameness, consistency, evenness. Following a set order, pattern, plan, etc. Although twelve-step fellowships emphasize unity and common purpose as the way to recovery, unity is not the same as uniformity. The rooms of twelve-step fellowships are filled with diverse groups of individuals who would ordinarily not get together, all trying to solve a common problem.

UNIQUE

One-of-a-kind, distinctive, rare. Something different or special from other things; out-of-the-ordinary. People in recovery (especially those new to the process) often feel unique, but not in a good way; they may feel themselves exempt from the workings and traditions of the twelve-step group or of life itself because of some special status, or they may feel unique in their isolation, or they may feel such shame and guilt over their past deeds, they are sure they are unique in all the world in their wrongdoings. Whatever the reason, feeling unique may be deadly for a recovering person. The phrase "terminal uniqueness" was coined to emphasize just how deadly feeling "unique" can be for a person trying to recover from addiction.

UNITY

Harmony, accord, unison. A spiritual principle. The state of being unified or united; being part of a cohesive group. In twelve-step terms, "unity of purpose" keeps the groups focused on the core problem the members are gathered to solve.

UNIVERSAL

Inclusive of all; total, entire. Having application to everyone, everywhere at all times. Spiritual principles are universal, and apply to everyone, everywhere, whether one realizes this or not.

UNMANAGEABILITY

Unable to be controlled, regulated, or ordered. Unmanageability may express itself in the life of an addict as job and marriage problems, arrests and incarcerations, serious debts, inability to pay bills, the inability to form and nurture relationships, etc.

UNREALISTIC EXPECTATIONS

Wants or desires regarding an outcome from a person, group, or particular situation that are not viable, that cannot be, or that would not be healthy if they came to pass. Placing demands or conditions on a person or situation that cannot be met; setting the stage for disappointment or resentment, which can be deadly for persons in recovery.

USELESSNESS

Ineffectiveness, inutility, inadequacy. Without purpose or direction. Individuals still in active addiction often report feeling hopeless, that their lives are meaningless or without any direction; they describe themselves as lost, confused, or depressed in active addiction. Living a life in recovery and especially being of service to others restores a feeling of usefulness to the life of a recovering person.

USER(S)

Consumer, not producer. People who use mind- and mood-altering chemicals. Can also refer to those who take advantage of other people or who are manipulative, using others to achieve their own ends. Similar to being a "taker" rather than a "giver."

USING

The act of taking into the body mind- and mood-altering chemicals or engaging in the behavior to which one is addicted. The act of fixating on a person, place, activity, or thing in order to fill a void inside the person that would otherwise be filled with a higher power.

USING DREAMS/DRUNK DREAMS

Dreams in which the dreamer experiences the sensations of being high, loaded, drunk, or engaged in addictive behavior. Settings may include old behaviors associated with using. They usually are not predictive or indicative of a deficiency in dreamer's program of recovery, such as a reservation.

VALUES

Principles, standards, morals. Also refers to ethics or ideals. Values may belong to a person or a group. Value can also mean "worth;" a person in recovery gives great worth to the concept of honesty; it is a value for that person.

VICES

Failings, faults, immoral behaviors or bad habits. Addiction itself is not a vice; it is a disease. Vices may be behaviors associated with the disease of addiction.

VIGILANCE

Watchfulness, attention, alertness. To be constantly and continually aware of situations, feelings, and behaviors that pose dangers to one's spiritual condition. Continuously working on recovery: praying, meditating, regularly attending meetings, etc. Self-monitoring to ensure adherence to one's program of recovery.

VULNERABLE

Susceptible, defenseless, weak. May be a feeling of being unprotected or at risk. Sharing or revealing intimate details about an individual with others. Allowing one to be open or transparent to another; putting one in a situation that could result in having one's behaviors or actions called into question. Paradoxically, one's attempts to hide or deny his or her vulnerabilities, instead of strengthening, often make him or her prone to relapse. By making oneself vulnerable, one often finds strength.

WE

The plural of "I;" or the first-person plural personal pronoun. Used when the speaker refers to him- or herself and others. The Twelve Steps of Narcotics Anonymous, adapted from the Twelve Steps of Alcoholics Anonymous, added the word "We" to the beginning of Steps One through Eleven, in order to emphasize that recovery is a "we" enterprise, not a solitary or isolated activity to be engaged in alone.

WELCOME

Salutation, receive, greeting. Used as a greeting given to newcomers and out-of-town visitors who identify themselves as such at meetings.

WILLINGNESS

Eagerness, enthusiasm, readiness. A key character asset or spiritual principle; said to be all that is required of a newcomer or old timer in working the program. The desire to complete a task and the decision to do whatever is necessary to accomplish it. Willingness gives those in recovery the ability to take action, to attend meetings, work steps, do service work, get and use a sponsor, and especially to be open-minded to the will of their higher power for their lives.

WILLPOWER

Determination, resolve, drive. Self-control or self-discipline.

WITHDRAWAL

Removal, extraction, departure. The physical, emotional, and psychological reaction the body experiences in the absence of a particular substance or combination of substances (detoxification). Takes place whether the substances used were prescribed or illicit (illegal/street) drugs, medications, or alcohol. May also accompany the cessation of an addictive behavior. Symptoms may include, but are not limited to: vomiting, nausea, aches, pains, seizures, headaches, sweats, and flu-like symptoms. May require hospitalization during the detoxification phase. This decision can be made by a medical doctor.

Withdrawal lasts varying amounts of time, depending on types of drugs used, combinations of drugs used, length of usage, health of the individual, and other factors.

Withdrawal generally occurs at the very beginning of recovery; only when all intoxicating substances and behaviors have been removed can the recovery process begin in earnest.

WINNER

Victor, champion, conqueror. One who does not give in to difficulties, but perseveres and continues to act upon spiritual principles, no matter who else is involved in the situation. People who do not use drugs or act on an addictive behavior. Winners are people who go to meetings regularly, work the Twelve Steps with a sponsor, volunteer for service work, help newcomers, and participate in other healthy, positive activities. Winners are those who strive to exemplify the characteristics of a healthy recovering person.

WISDOM

Knowledge, insight, good judgment. May be learned or gained from one's own past personal experiences or by observing and learning from the collective experiences of others.

WORRY

Anxiety, stress, fear. Discomfort or unease. Mental distress. Projection of a given or feared outcome. To be overwhelmed with concerns so much so that they interfere with daily activities. Worry should be avoided by persons in recovery as much as possible. Sharing concerns with a sponsor is one way to drain worries of their power. Sharing at group level or with recovery friends is also helpful.

WORTH

Importance, value, significance. The merit or significance of a thing; be it concrete or abstract. One's recovery is worth any amount of time or effort.

WORTHWHILE

Important, meaningful, valuable. Deserving of the time and effort spent on it, like one's recovery.

WORTHY

Admirable, commendable, praiseworthy. The quality or state of being deserving. Persons newly in recovery may feel they are not worthy of the love and friendship of the other members of the fellowship, but after some time, and especially while living by the principles of the Twelve Steps and performing commendable actions such as being of service, one usually begins to realize one is worthy of recovery despite everything.

WRITING PROCESS

The method of working the Twelve Steps by answering questions about them, writing one's thoughts about and understandings of them in one's journal or notebook, done under the guidance of a sponsor. The act of listing and describing feelings, thoughts, ideas, etc. on paper and then reading what one has written to a sponsor or another guide through the Twelve Steps. Writing is an important part of twelve-step recovery.

WRONGS (WRONGDOINGS)

Crimes, injuries, wounds. The hurtful and/or injurious things one has done to others; what others have suffered because of one's active addiction. These are what the Ninth Step amends process is designed to address.

ZEAL

Passion, enthusiasm, gusto. Excitement and eagerness for something; a cause, a belief, a way of life, etc. The feeling one has for one's program of recovery that causes one to embrace the twelve-step way of life enthusiastically.

Meeting and Fellowship Etiquette

Going to the first meeting of any twelve-step program can be a terrifying, confusing, and sometimes paralyzing experience. A person attending a meeting for the first time can take comfort in knowing that *each and every person* at the meeting had to go through the same experience of walking into that room for the first time. Every member or potential member faced the fear of identifying him- or herself as an addict, alcoholic, overeater, compulsive gambler, codependent, sex and love addict, and then taking that first key tag or chip. Regardless of the length of clean time, recovery, sobriety, or abstinence, there was a time when every single person at that meeting had only one day. That is, perhaps, the most important thing to remember.

There are ways to make the experience a little easier. "Meeting and Fellowship Etiquette" is intended as an easy guide to help you understand what to expect when you walk through the door of your first meeting and what to do while you're there. We hope this guide will be useful for both newcomer and old timer alike. Showing respect for each group, listening to the members of that group, and following the meeting format will help any newcomer (or old timer) have an enjoyable meeting experience.

What is Meeting Etiquette?

Meeting etiquette consists of customs, manners, and propriety; it is the way to conduct oneself while in a recovery meeting. Meeting and fellowship etiquette has become an important topic among many members of the twelve-step community, as well as those who refer people to the various twelve-step programs. People "associated," but not "affiliated" with twelve-step recovery, such as judges, law enforcement and medical professionals, and others are taking an increasing interest in what actually happens to a newcomer being sent to his or her first meeting. These professionals want to ensure that any newcomer is treated with respect and that those people they refer to meetings are not taken advantage of. They also want to ensure that the meetings actually provide those services as presented in the public relations material from various twelve-step service bodies.

Meeting etiquette has traditionally been a concept passed down from one recovering person to another, e.g., from sponsor to sponsee or a more experienced member to the newer member. There is no standard or accepted model beyond what is written in the Twelve Traditions; however, it is common for each member to take personal responsibility for his or her own fellowship and to make certain that there is an atmosphere of recovery found in the meetings. Most "violations" of meeting etiquette are usually addressed by more long-standing members of a group, usually in a kind and tolerant way.

Examples of meeting etiquette are as follows:

- Getting to a meeting early enables an attendee to get a beverage, use the restroom, socialize, etc., so they can:
  - › Be sure of a seat before the meeting begins;
  - › Avoid the disruption of performing these activities while members are reading or sharing.

- Leaving and returning to one's seat or speaking to one's neighbors during the meeting is frowned upon, as this distracts those who may be sharing or those attempting to pay attention.

- If asked to read one of the passages or literature selections, it is considered respectful to read them as written, without adding comments or "sound effects." The literature of each twelve-step program was written with great care to be of help to those who suffer. It was voted on by group conscience and each fellowship as a body agreed on the final presentation. Anyone with a disagreement on a particular reading should simply excuse him- or herself from reading it aloud and discuss it afterward, privately, with a sponsor or other program member. "Editorial comments" or "callbacks" in a meeting might confuse or alarm newcomers or others who desperately need to hear the message of recovery as it was intended.

- Using only the language and literature consistent with the twelve-step meeting you are attending ensures that a clear message of recovery is being offered. Using mixed language from various fellowships sends mixed messages and can cause newer members to be confused about the meeting's primary purpose.

- The guideline against "cross-talking" or "sniper sharing" (see pages 162-163) helps maintain a calm and safe atmosphere of recovery in the meetings.

- "Stay in the meeting from prayer to prayer." Since most meetings begin and end with a prayer, "staying in the meeting from prayer to prayer" means both physical attendance and mental focus on the meeting from beginning to end.

- The Seventh Tradition states that groups should be fully self-supporting and decline outside contributions. This allows twelve-step groups to carry the message the way it was intended, without the influence of outside people or organizations. It is customary to put a contribution in the basket if one can afford to, but it is not required, nor it is appropriate for a visitor (or newcomer in the first thirty days of recovery, in some fellowships).

- Members do not publicly mention specific facilities, treatment centers, detoxification units, hospitals, halfway houses, etc. Doing so is considered an implied endorsement of these facilities/entities by the member. This is especially important if a member serves on an area or regional public information service body. As such, the member is viewed by the public as a representative of his or her fellowship and will think that the fellowship, rather than the member, is endorsing a specific entity.

- Members refer to the meeting by its name rather than the facility where it is held. Referring to a facility may imply a relationship with the facility.

- Members refrain from mentioning specific drugs or tell overly detailed "war stories" ("drunkalogues" or "drugalogues"); it can make others in the meeting uncomfortable if specific drugs or excessive details are mentioned.

- Many groups will ask members to keep their sharing between three to five minutes in order to give everyone who wishes to share a chance to do so. This is especially important if the meeting has a large number of members in attendance.

- Members show respect for the facility where the meeting is held. Twelve-step programs may not be affiliated with the facility, but they have a responsibility to make certain that the meeting area is left in as good a condition or better than it was found. Smokers should dispose of cigarette butts in an appropriate manner, using cigarette receptacles or ashtrays. Be mindful of behavior outside the meeting as well; negative complaints from neighbors to the facility is a direct reflection on the twelve-step group and has caused many groups to lose a meeting place. Many meetings are held in public places. Groups want to make sure that the behavior of a few members does not negatively affect the fellowship as a whole.

If someone is being disrespectful or placing the meeting location in jeopardy, then it is usually the responsibility of the chairperson or secretary to bring the issue to that person's attention. However, no person has the power or authority to berate, reprimand, or expel another from a twelve-step program. They can ask an individual not to return to a particular group or facility if chronic negative behavior puts the facility or its members at risk. The meeting secretary has a responsibility to approach the disruptive person and explain, in a respectful manner, why or why not a certain practice is unacceptable.

FAQs and General Program Facts

The following are some of the more common questions and more detailed answers about attending meetings. There are many more questions and far more answers than space permits, but this is intended as a good start (and good refresher) for people attending a meeting of any twelve-step program.

How do I identify/What do I say?

You've almost certainly heard the formula, in movies or on TV: "Hello, my name is X, and I'm a Y." If you are attending a meeting for the first time, pay attention to what other people are saying and try to imitate them. As a general rule, you do not need to identify as "something AND something," for example as "an addict AND an alcoholic," regardless of whether you are attending Alcoholics Anonymous or Narcotics Anonymous. In either program it is usually considered disrespectful. Naturally, there are a variety of opinions on this subject, but generally speaking, the leadership of both organizations would probably agree that if you are in NA, you should say "addict" and identify your amount of time in the program as "clean time" or "recovery." If you are attending AA, you should say "alcoholic" and identify your amount of time in the program as "sobriety."

Where do I sit?

Many people will encourage you to sit in the front of the room. It is best to sit in a place where you can focus on the leader of the meeting and not be distracted. Some meetings will fill up from front-to-back, while others will fill back-to-front. Many meetings in urban or densely populated areas are standing-room-only after a certain time, so get to the meeting early and get a seat. It is generally accepted to save a couple of seats until the meeting fills up. If people are standing or looking for seats close to the start time, common courtesy says you should give up the saved seat(s). Remember, getting to a meeting early enough to get a seat is the responsibility of the program member; they will understand why you could not hold a seat indefinitely.

Can I go outside during the meeting? Do I need to stay for the whole thing?

There's a saying—"the only meeting you're ever late for is your first one." Of course, it's best to arrive early, but many programs believe it is better to arrive late to a meeting than not at all. In smaller meetings it may be more noticeable if you arrive late, but it is completely normal and accepted to come into a meeting late. Just remember that a meeting *is* going on and try not to be distracting. If you need to leave the meeting early, simply gather your things and, if absolutely necessary, quietly excuse yourself to your immediate neighbors.

How long do I need to stay in the meeting?

The general rule is, "prayer to prayer." If you really want the full benefit of the experience, then you should stay from the opening prayer to the closing prayer. Most people in recovery will also say, "Get there early and stay late." Much of what happens in recovery takes place before and after the meeting, during the informal period of "fellowshipping." It's the best way for people to get to know you and for you get to know other recovering people.

Meeting attendance or court cards

If you have an attendance or court card requiring a signature, place it in the basket when it is passed for the Seventh Tradition. Usually the meeting secretary or treasurer will sign it and then make it available to you after the meeting has ended. This is done as a courtesy to you; the group is not required to sign your card. Please wait until the end of the meeting to get your card back. And never interrupt the meeting by trying to get a meeting attendance card signed for a meeting that you intend to leave early.

Sharing and introductions

At the beginning of some meetings (usually closed meetings and not often in very large meetings) everyone in the room will take turns to introduce themselves. Other than that, it is always common practice for the person who shares to introduce him- or herself by saying his or her first name and identifying in the way that is accepted by that group or program, as in, "My name is Jane, and I am an [addict, alcoholic, compulsive gambler, etc.]." In most cases, you do not need to identify with more than one disease. It is redundant and unnecessary to say "addict and alcoholic" for example. If you are an addict, it includes alcohol. If you are at an AA meeting the reason for your attendance is to address your use of alcohol and not other drugs.

If you are asked to identify yourself at your first meeting and are not yet comfortable with that identification, you can simply say your name and that you are not sure you have a problem and that you came to the meeting to learn more. You will be welcome to stay either way.

At some meetings, group members will also acknowledge their recovery date or the date on which their recovery began, such as, "My name is John and I'm an addict with four years clean." This, however, is usually more common in newcomer groups or therapeutic groups that are not twelve-step oriented.

Sharing

You (usually) will only be asked to share at a meeting if you have been abstinent for at least twenty-four hours. Don't be offended if you are not asked to share immediately at your first meeting; the members may have noted your nervousness as a newcomer (after all, each of them was in your seat, once), and they may be respecting your need to "feel better" before they ask you to share.

A newcomer may not be called on for another reason; the program members may wish to hear about recovery and until you have some time under your belt, you can't say very much about that subject. Often newcomers will share about events in their past while loaded, since that is basically all they have to share. While sharing such is certainly not verboten, most meetings have formats that focus on recovery and talking about your alcohol or drug use just isn't that interesting to most individuals in recovery. In time, however, most people who want to do so get a chance to share.

No cross-talk.

"Cross talk" is speaking directly to a person who has shared in a meeting and offering advice to them during the meeting. This is another way that twelve-step meetings differ from group therapy. Most consider cross-talk to be unacceptable. In general, people do not share their honest thoughts and feelings in a meeting so that others present can comment, jeer, debate, heckle, or otherwise offer their personal opinions on what a person just shared. If people were permitted to remark on each other's sharing, the meeting could very easily become sidetracked, and the primary purpose—recovery—forgotten. Members often enjoy each other's company and like to talk about many subjects, and even tease each other and mention what was shared, but after, not during a meeting.

It is inappropriate to make abusive, racist, sexist comments, or to share in such crude ways as to offend others in the room. If you do so you may be asked not to share again.

Your sponsor or program friends will undoubtedly let you know if your sharing was inappropriate; more often, other members may approach you after the meeting to compliment you on what you shared! Either way, it usually is done in the spirit of helping and fellowship.

What if you want to go to a meeting to "check things out" for yourself or a friend or you are just not quite sure that you have a problem?

Find an open meeting. Most meetings will be described in program schedules as either "open" or "closed." If you call a central office or hotline number, ask the person who answers the phone to guide you. A meeting that is listed as open is considered open to anyone who wants to attend. These open meetings are usually where family members or friends attend with their loved one who is in recovery. Open meeting also are meetings where people who are unsure if they have a problem can find more information about how to make an informed decision.

Do I have to stop: using, drinking, gambling, spending, shopping, smoking, having sex, being compulsive, or codependent, etc. before I can attend a meeting?

No, but it *is* strongly suggested that you do not bring with you any drugs, paraphernalia, or any items considered a threat to the members of the fellowship you are attending; however, if you do show up to a meeting loaded or drunk, no one will ask you to leave unless you are also being belligerent or seem extremely ill. Remember, the people in the meeting may be clean or sober now, but they have experience being around those who are still in active addiction. You will not frighten them or make them want to use. You are not that powerful.

Are there leaders or bosses at groups or meetings?

No, but most meetings do have a secretary or chairperson (called trusted servants) who sets up the room, hands out readings, and/or finds speakers for the meeting. These trusted servants are not serving in any official or corporate capacity; rather, they are elected by other group members and are willing to serve the group. All service positions in twelve-step programs are voluntary, and members serve on a rotating schedule.

Starting a group or meeting

Be sure to consider a few things before you start a meeting: Is there a need for a meeting in your area/vicinity? Have you been in contact with your area service committee? Have you researched a meeting location and what the costs would be? Do you have a fellow addict who can help support the meeting as it gets off the ground? Most area service committees in the various twelve-step fellowships have a literature distribution subcommittee and often help new meetings by providing a group starter kit that contains information pamphlets, group readings, and/or key tags. These fellowships also can provide helpful information about starting a meeting or group.

Prayers at meetings

Most twelve-step meetings usually will open and close with a prayer. These prayers are not intended to promote any particular sect or denomination of any particular faith, though some of them may sound familiar to you. The "Lord's Prayer" is commonly heard at AA meetings, while at NA and GA meetings it is generally not. Some prayers will have the word "God" in them, but this is generally meant as the God of one's own understanding and not meant to denote a specific denomination.

What is the difference between meetings and groups?

A group can be defined as a gathering of two or more persons who come together for the specific purpose of sharing their recovery from addiction or other manifestation of addiction with other persons in recovery. Meetings usually take place at a regularly scheduled time and location. A group may include newcomers and "regulars" or members who have been attending the same meeting together for some time. A group essentially sponsors or organizes a meeting; a group usually has a name and adheres to an agreed-upon format (speaker, book study, open discussion, etc.). Groups may coalesce around a common theme or membership feature; hence, there may be gay groups, women's groups, men's stag groups, old timers groups, young people's groups, and so on.

What is a home group?

Persons seeking recovery are welcome to attend any meeting of whichever fellowship addresses their particular problem, whether AA, NA, GA, OA, SLAA, or so on. However, most people find it important to "belong" to one particular group, which they call their "home group." Some fellowships strongly recommend home group membership and service.

In the home group the recovering person finds friendship (fellowship) and may accept service responsibilities. Home group members attend business meetings of the group, organize special events for the group, and help set up and clean up after meetings. The home group is often simply the group within which the recovering person feels most comfortable; sometimes a home group is chosen because it is the group a person's sponsor belongs to.

Typical service positions in a home group include secretary or chairperson, treasurer, group representative, coffee person, literature person, greeter, and other positions. The secretary or chairperson is usually responsible for selecting members who will then lead the meeting; a secretary may make announcements, share, open and close the meeting, and make sure other service positions are fulfilled.

There also are elected positions, filled by members of the group at what is called a "business meeting" or "steering meeting" that is usually held once a month. At these meetings, any monies collected by the group over and above what is needed for rent and coffee, are banked or otherwise earmarked by group conscience to make a contribution to the next level of service, such as area service committee, regional service committee, and/or world services.

Atmosphere of recovery

Each meeting can be as different as the members in it. Some meetings are more social, standing-room-only types of meetings, while others are more serious, intimate, or quiet. Some meetings are somber and focused, while others may be more genial and comradely. Whatever the type of meeting, an atmosphere of recovery is established and maintained by a few rules. These generally include a ban on the overt use of cell phones or other communication devices (even in a silent mode, for texting), dissuasion against private conversations during sharing, and a request that all in attendance respect the needs of the group. Remember, members are dealing with life-and-death issues, and some of the attendees may be very fragile and need to be able to hear what the speakers are sharing.

The norms of the group will usually become evident, whether lenient or strict. Also contributing to the atmosphere of recovery is respect for the meeting facility and acknowledgement that the actions of any particular group are a reflection on the twelve-step program as a whole. One disrespectful group may spoil a meeting location for other groups, and since most twelve-step groups operate on a basis of "attraction, not promotion," bad behavior might prove a "turnoff" to someone who sorely needs the program, but who is repelled by what he or she perceives as the values of the group.

Special interest or common needs meetings

Most programs have some meetings that are specifically targeted at certain populations. These may be established for men only, women only, gay, lesbian, bisexual, and transgender (GLBT) only, young people only, or professionals. Each type of meeting calls for special notice of its own membership and practices. A few examples of special interest or common needs meetings are:

- **Stag (Men's or Women's) Meetings**
  "Stag" (gender-specific) groups provide an opportunity for men to share about feelings and behaviors they would feel awkward discussing in front of women and vice versa. These meetings also

provide opportunities for women to find women sponsors and men to do likewise with men. Much bonding and fellowshipping is possible in these same-sex meetings (sometimes called "buddying-up"). If you find yourself in a meeting for the opposite gender, don't be offended if you are redirected to another meeting; on the other hand, you may be invited to stay, for that one meeting at least.

◆ GLBT Meetings

GLBT meetings originated in part as a result of AIDS; in the early years of the epidemic, many, if not most of those infected with the virus were gay, and of course those gay addicts and alcoholics wanted to share at meetings about this terrible disease and its impact on their lives. There's still debate as to whether it was fear of the disease or plain bigotry that led heterosexual program members to insist that sharing about AIDS was an "outside issue," but whatever the reason, GLBT alcoholics and addicts branched out and formed their own groups where they could discuss their special fears and concerns, as well as their recovery.

◆ Young People's Meetings

There is not a clear definition of how old a "young" person should be, but as more facts becomes known about addiction, people are no longer waiting until middle age to enter recovery; it's not uncommon for teenagers to have multiple years in a program. An acceptable age for a "young person" at a meeting so specified would be from about mid-teens to late twenties.

◆ Professional Meetings

In some twelve-step fellowships, there may be certain meetings not on any official schedule. These undisclosed meetings may be for professionals such as doctors, lawyers, politicians, nurses, and/or celebrities whose livelihood depends on an even greater degree of anonymity than that practiced in regular twelve-step meetings.

Meeting formats

Even within the various fellowships, there are different formats for twelve-step meetings. The names and descriptions will vary depending on geographic locations, local customs, and the differences in twelve-step programs. The descriptions below offer a general overview. Meeting directories and Internet sites usually will have a legend to direct you to the meeting type you want to attend.

Open Meetings are open to anyone who wants to attend, including family, friends, or members of the public who are simply interested in getting more information about the program.

Closed Meetings are only for people who are members of the program or who have the desire to stop using or acting on their addiction.

Newcomer Meetings focus on specific issues that are common to those who are new to the twelve-step program and the recovery process. Issues may be: finding a sponsor, establishing a meeting habit, or celebrating milestones in early recovery.

Speaker Meetings feature one or more members who share their experiences by telling the story of what active addiction was like, what early recovery was like, and what their life is like now. These shares vary in length depending on the meeting and may last anywhere from fifteen to forty-five minutes, sometimes followed by question-and-answer or open participation from others in attendance at the meeting.

Step (or Tradition) Study Meetings as the name suggests, focus on a specific step or tradition at each meeting. Text regarding the step or tradition being studied is usually read aloud from approved program literature, the leader or chairperson discusses his or her interpretation or experience with that step, and sharing may or may not follow, which could include a question-and-answer session.

Discussion or Open Participation Meetings have a leader or chairperson who starts the meeting off with a general share of a few minutes, then selects a topic, and then either calls on people to share or acknowledges volunteers who wish to speak. Sharing happens in a variety of ways at any given meeting, including the raising of hands, calling out at the end of another's share, "tag" meetings where at the end of his or her sharing, the speaker calls on the next person (sometimes called Monterey-style sharing), and so on. The format of the meeting will usually be announced at the beginning. Some meetings appoint members who act as timers to make sure that one person does not dominate/monopolize the sharing so that all who wish to may participate.

Book Study refers to reading the program's literature, including, but not limited to, its primary text and additional conference-approved literature.

Candlelight Meetings are those held by candlelight. The dim lighting is thought to make it easier for some people to share and contributes to an atmosphere of calmness and serenity.

Getting "kicked out" of a meeting

As a general rule, you cannot get "kicked out" of a twelve-step program. You can, however, be asked to leave a meeting place or location because you are not following group or facility rules. If you are asked to leave a meeting location by the secretary or elected representative of the group, you are obligated to leave that space. A law enforcement official could be called in and a charge of trespassing pressed. This is an extreme situation, but may be necessary, and if so, is well within the legal rights of a group and its trusted servants.

How to Find Meetings

You can check the websites or phone numbers of the program you are interested in for the most up-to-date information before contacting any of the locations or addresses listed below. If the number is no longer valid, you can also contact directory assistance in your local area. Most twelve-step programs also have local helpline numbers that you can obtain through contacting directory assistance or by looking in a phone book. Your doctor or clergyperson may also be able to refer you.

It is important to know these phone numbers are not crisis hotlines. In most cases the phones are either answered by volunteers or employees (special workers) who are not, in any case, professional counselors. For emergencies, always call 9-1-1 or the local emergency number in your area.

AL-ANON & ALATEEN
Al-Anon Family Group Headquarters, Inc.
1600 Corporate Landing Parkway
Virginia Beach, VA 23454-5617
Tel: (757) 563-1600
www.al-anon.alateen.org

ALCOHOLICS ANONYMOUS
General Service Office, A
World Services, Inc.
P.O. Box 459
New York, NY 10163
Tel: (212) 870-3400
www.aa.org

CODEPENDENTS ANONYMOUS
CoDA, Fellowship Services Office
P.O. Box 33577
Phoenix, AZ 85067-3577
Tel: (602) 277-7991
www.codependents.org

DEBTORS ANONYMOUS
General Service Office
P.O. Box 920888
Needham, MA 02492-0009
Tel: (800)-421-2383
www.debtorsanonymous.org

GAMBLERS ANONYMOUS
International Service Office
P.O. Box 17173
Los Angeles, CA 90017
Tel: (213) 386-8789
www.gamblersanonymous.org

NAR-ANON

Nar-Anon Family Group Headquarters, Inc.
22527 Crenshaw Blvd, #200B
Torrance, CA 90505
Tel: (800) 477-6291
www.nar-anon.org

NARCOTICS ANONYMOUS

World Service Office, NA World Services, Inc.
P.O. Box 9999
Van Nuys, California 91409 USA
Tel: (818) 773-9999
www.na.org

OVEREATERS ANONYMOUS

World Service Office
P.O. Box 44020
Rio Rancho, NM 87174-4020
Tel: (505) 891-2664
www.oa.org

SEX AND LOVE ADDICTS ANONYMOUS

Fellowship-Wide Services Office
1550 NE Loop 410, Ste 118
San Antonio, TX 78209
Tel: (210) 828-7900
www.slaafws.org

Slogans of Recovery

Introduction

"Easy Does It," "Ninety in Ninety," "Suit up and Show up," "Focus on the Message, not the Messenger"; these and other slogans abound in twelve-step programs and meetings. Each meeting is different and there are tremendous differences depending on what part of the country (or world) a person may attend a meeting. Some of the slogans and phrases are fairly common regardless of where someone may attend a meeting, while others are only heard in a handful of programs or certain select cities or states or countries. Sometimes these slogans or mottos are printed up in fancy type, framed, and hung on the walls of meeting rooms. A newcomer often may feel confused, overwhelmed, or even disdainful on encountering these seemingly simple-minded slogans. So what do they all mean? That's what this introduction aims to explain.

This section on "Slogans of Recovery" is by no means a complete or comprehensive list, but it should provide a reference or starting point for understanding these shorthand messages from twelve-step experience. Use these slogans as you would anything else you hear in a meeting; come up with a meaning that works for you and disregard what doesn't. Your understanding is sure to grow deeper as you immerse yourself in your chosen fellowship and work the Twelve Steps.

› **90 meetings in 90 days; 90-in-90.** Newcomers are encouraged to attend one twelve-step meeting every day for a period of at least ninety days. This enables the newcomer to meet people within his or her selected fellowship, as well as potential sponsors, become familiar with the program and the Twelve Steps, and develop a new habit of attending meetings.

› **A meeting a day keeps the detox away.** Those who attend meetings regularly tend to have a higher success rate than those who do not. Newcomers are encouraged to attend a meeting a day for at least the first ninety days of their recovery, and although there is no mandated minimum number of meetings for newcomers or old timers, frequent meeting attendance contributes to long-term recovery.

› **A new way of life.** "The Twelve Steps have shown me a new way of life." This phrase is often heard at twelve-step meetings and is really just a different way of living the same life, but performing different actions, and having different perceptions, even while living in the same home, family, or job situation. The person in recovery changes, even if all the circumstances of his or her life do not.

› **An addict alone is in bad company.** The essence of twelve-step programs is experienced when one person in recovery talks to or works with another, whether one-on-one or in a group. Many people in recovery find it easier to talk with someone who has personal experience with addressing the feelings and other manifestations of addiction rather than talking with a professional, such as a therapist, psychiatrist, or clerical person. But because people tended to isolate while in active addiction, it can be difficult for them, once in recovery, to seek the company and counsel of others in the program. This slogan reminds them that it's important to do so. When someone in recovery is alone, old thoughts and feelings can surface, along with the conviction that getting loaded might be a good idea.

› **Anger is fear in a party dress.** In the recovery community it is generally accepted that the basis of most anger is fear. Addressing the root fear usually gets to the root of anger.

> **Atmosphere of recovery.** The physical and emotional environment of the twelve-step meeting should be such that it promotes recovery, security, welcome, and acceptance in order to engender hope, especially for newcomers. An atmosphere of recovery is warm, friendly, and takes into account the fear that newcomers or those returning from relapse might be experiencing.

> **Building a foundation.** Learning the basics of the program, from frequent meeting attendance, to getting a sponsor, to using the phone, to reading program literature, to beginning to work the steps is all part of building a foundation in recovery. On that foundation the member will be able to build a new life. The fundamentals of the program are said to give members the tools to face problems associated with normal, everyday routines that used to seem too challenging or difficult.

> **By the grace of God/There, but for the grace of God, (go I).** These sayings are frequently heard and sound confusingly alike. Both are based in a traditional Judeo-Christian theology; members who are atheist, agnostic, new-age, or followers of Eastern philosophies might instead believe (for example) that personal responsibility is the deciding factor between relapse and recovery.

The first saying, "by the grace of God," indicates that the speaker believes that he or she did not actually cause his or her own good fortune (such as his or her recovery), but that whatever good came to him or her was a freely given gift, or *grace*, from the God of his or her understanding or his or her higher power.

The second, "there, but for the grace of God, (go I)," is frequently used when discussing the misfortune of another. One member's relapse might be cause for concern among the other members of the group who might refer to it in a meeting, not as a matter of gossip, but as a troubling event they are trying to process. In doing so, a clean/sober/abstinent member might remark, "there, but for the grace of God, go I," indicating that he or she credits his or her higher power with keeping him or her clean/sober/abstinent, coupled with the realization that anyone, including him- or herself, can also relapse. No one is immune.

› **Call your sponsor.** Pick up the telephone and ask for help working the Twelve Steps. A person to whom this is said might be showing signs of being in denial or acting out in some way and may be in need of having another's perspective, particularly that of his or her sponsor.

› **Carry the message.** From the Twelfth Step, this refers to a member being an example in action, as well as word for others seeking recovery. It also refers to sharing, either personally or at a group level, about one's life and recovery experiences. The message referred to is that any individual can stop using/drinking/acting out/etc. by embracing and practicing the principles embodied in the Twelve Steps and, by doing so, start to enjoy a life free of addiction.

› **Cash-register honesty:** Honesty in deed as well as in word; when given too much change, a person with "cash-register honesty" promptly calls the mistake to the cashier's attention and returns it, instead of pocketing it. Practicing cash-register honesty is part of working a good program.

› **Change (or Recovery) is a process, not an event.** Most people with the disease of addiction seem to be more interested in instant gratification rather than in long-term investments of time and effort that will bear fruit some time in the future. This saying is intended to remind them that recovery is a life-long process that will bring benefits as long as the recovering person makes the efforts recommended by the program. The point is that one doesn't simply discontinue a certain behavior and, then "ta-da," achieve recovery!

Recovery can be thought of as a bank account of sorts that a recovering person invests in each time he or she goes to a meeting, works the steps, calls his or her sponsor, meditates, prays, works with a newcomer, answers the phone when another person in need calls, or stays clean/sober/etc. another day. This "bank account" is something the person may access in times of need, when issues come up, or when he or she has a bad day. Those in recovery never know when they will need to draw on that reserve; but when that day comes, there must be assets in the account.

› **Circuit speaker:** A circuit speaker is a program member with a gift for public speaking and a charismatic way of "pitching" their experience in recovery. They travel at the invitation of local groups and may speak all across the country and around the world.

Some circuit speakers become so sought-after or venerated, problems of ego and hero-worship can arise; additionally, some members feel that circuit speakers can sound "stale" or "canned" after telling their story so many times. However, many a newcomer has been inspired by a circuit speaker, and hearing a speaker with an entertaining or inspiring story may be just what a newcomer or other member needs to stay clean/sober/etc. one more day.

› **Conference-approved literature:** Written material used in meetings and published or approved by the international or national service body of that program. Material that is not approved by the conference (or fellowship) is not distributed at meetings. Books and materials written by other organizations are generally not sold or used in twelve-step meetings.

› **Don't quit five minutes before the miracle happens.** It's often the case that a person in recovery becomes discouraged and "gives up" right before a breakthrough or solution to a problem occurs (the "miracle"). Those around that person, who have more time in recovery, often recognize that this is about to happen and counsels the sufferer not to give up with these words.

A recovering individual may stop working the program, claiming discouragement, in order to avoid doing some of the hard work of recovery. A sponsor or program friend who understands this and uses this quote might be just the encouragement a person needs to break through to the next level of recovery.

> **Easy does it.** Advice for working every component of a twelve-step program. Since most people in recovery are often "extremists," it's not uncommon for them to want to suddenly master every aspect of their newfound program and fellowship, including their own lives. This is a recipe for disaster. Old timers know that the best way to approach any problem is a bit at a time, not all at once. It is a formula that in many ways defies reason that even the founders of Alcoholics Anonymous did not fully understand. The only thing that is known for sure is that the steps work as they are written. When asked how the steps really work, co-founder Bill W said once in an interview, "Slowly."

> **Enjoy life; this is not a dress rehearsal.** Living in the moment or living just for today is the goal of recovery. Learning to appreciate the daily experience rather than dwelling in the past or projecting into the future is considered the key to freedom and peace of mind. Happiness, joy, and serenity are only possible in the present.

> **Experience is what you get when you don't get what you want.** A response to a member who believes his or her prayer wasn't answered. If the desired outcome was not "delivered," then the person who prayed has the opportunity to learn some lessons, including how to deal with disappointment and remain in recovery.

> **Focus on the message, not the messenger.** It is really easy at a meeting (especially after attending regularly for an extended period of time) to focus on the person who is sharing rather than what is being shared. So this saying encourages one to listen to what is being said, rather than judging the person saying it. Usually, it is the most unlikely person who delivers the most important message.

> **Focus on the similarities and not the differences, or Identify, don't compare.** Denial has killed many people seeking recovery—the feeling that one is different prevents many from accepting the help of a twelve-step program and allows continued using or acting out. Once an individual accepts that he or she has more similarities to than differences from other program members, recovery can begin.

› **Friend of Bill:** A member of Alcoholics Anonymous. In order to maintain anonymity and avoid giving offense, upon meeting someone for the first time, a member of AA might ask "are you a friend of Bill?" If the person is an AA member, he or she will recognize the meaning of the question and can answer yes; if not, no harm has been done.

› **Getting back to the basics:** The basics are the fundamentals of twelve-step programs that include obtaining, calling, and using a sponsor; working the Twelve Steps with that sponsor; attending meetings regularly; fulfilling some sort of service commitment at a group level; and reaching out to others in the program through sharing, calling, or listening to others in recovery. When a recovering person drifts or gets complacent, he or she may have stopped doing the basics of recovery. This often happens because that person has family, school, or work obligations of his or her "new life" and forgets to do the simple things that made that new life possible in the first place. When people in recovery get too far from doing the basics necessary to maintain recovery, they may not be prepared when "life on life's terms" presents itself. Either they will have enough of a foundation to get back to working the program the way they should, or they may relapse.

› **Getting better doesn't always feel better.** The process of working the Twelve Steps, admitting powerlessness, opening one's mind, taking an inventory, looking at character defects, making amends, taking regular personal inventory, engaging in prayer and meditation, and trying to help others are often challenging and may cause disturbances in the familiar cycle of one's own life and thinking, while restructuring one's life and priorities. This restructuring can cause pain or discomfort, as in working out at the gym, for example. "No pain, no gain," is another way to express this concept.

› **Gift of despair/gift of desperation:** The experience of "hitting bottom," with its inescapable shame, degradation, pain, and loss is, in retrospect, often viewed by those in recovery as having been a gift, in that it was the thing that finally stopped them and brought them into recovery.

> **GOD equals Good Orderly Direction.** As early as Step Two, people in recovery are confronted with the need to believe that something (a power) greater than themselves not only exists, but can bring about a profound change in their lives. The word God itself is repeated several times throughout the rest of the steps. This may present a problem for those individuals who are atheists or who have rejected the idea of God. Thinking of God as "Good Orderly Direction," rather than as the deity of a particular religion, helps skeptics, agnostics, and atheists, as well as those who still may have difficulty with the God of their childhood, to practice the steps and follow the program.

> **Guilt is the gift that keeps on giving.** Guilt can be viewed as a gift when it provides a recovering person with the motivation to change. The fear or apprehension of feeling guilt can sometimes motivate an individual to continue to practice principles in all of his or her affairs. In that sense, guilt (like desperation) may often be a gift to a recovering person.

> **HALT(S): Hungry, Angry, Lonely, Tired, (being too Serious)**: Any of these five states affecting one's mental, physical, and emotional well-being are believed to make a recovering individual vulnerable to relapse. Asking if someone in recovery is feeling any of these sensations or emotions is a quick way to evaluate whether it is time to put a "HALT(S)" to what he or she is doing, call his or her sponsor, and go to a meeting.

> **Higher-Powered:** A play on the words "higher power," lightheartedly announcing that one is energized by a power higher or greater than oneself.

> **I can't; we can.** The basis of the twelve-step program model is the healing benefits derived from one recovering individual helping another recovering individual. What one cannot accomplish alone, two or more can do together.

› **I may not be much, but I'm all I think about.** Self-deprecating humorous recognition by someone in recovery that he or she is being self-centered and/or self-obsessed. Regardless of how it manifests, addiction is all-consuming and those people who suffer from it are frequently only concerned with themselves while actively using. This self-centeredness does not simply vanish when the person stops using, drinking, or acting on a behavior. This expression is an ironic admission that an individual in recovery is aware of this defect.

› *I'll* **drink poison to make** *you* **sick.** To cling to resentment against another does nothing to the other; instead, it harms the person holding onto resentment. Holding onto resentments is usually why an individual will not go to a certain meeting or other fellowship gatherings/functions and this is dangerous because it can isolate and alienate the individual.

› **If I don't change, my clean/sober/abstinent date will.** If a person who comes into recovery does not change his or her behavior and lifestyles, then he or she will most likely relapse. If he or she is lucky enough to make it back into the program, it will be with a new recovery date.

› **If you are in the center, it's harder to fall off the edge.** It is considered important to recovery and the recovery process to put oneself in the "middle of the herd," that is, in the middle of the recovery community. To stay on the edge of recovery or the recovery community puts one at risk of being vulnerable to using or returning to old behavior in difficult and/or challenging times. Think of animals who move in packs; those on the edges are at greater risk of being "picked off" by predators than those in the middle of the herd.

› **If you are too busy to pray, you are too busy.** People who make time to pray and center themselves usually find more peace and balance in recovery. A life in recovery that has no time in it for prayer may end in relapse. Making the time to pray and/or meditate adds value to all other activities.

> **If you do what you always did, you'll get what you always got.** The recovery process is all about change. The concept of doing something different does not only apply to someone who is new in recovery. There will be times when a person with long-term recovery is just not satisfied with what they are getting out of life or recovery. In such cases, it is important for that person to do something different (within the twelve-step program) if he or she wants to get something different out of life.

> **If you don't have a home group, you are homeless.** A home group runs the meeting that a recovering person attends most frequently, where he or she has commitments, and at least some friends who will notice if he or she is absent, unhappy, or ill. Having a home group offers a life line for many people in recovery, making them feel part of and finding support when needed. Being accountable to one's home group is important; lack of accountability (not just to a home group) can set the stage for relapse.

> **If you don't pick up, you won't get loaded./If you don't drink, you won't get drunk.** Members fear relapsing or reverting to an old behavior because for some, a relapse means certain death. While there are many things a recovering person must do for his or her recovery, the most important and primary action is to not use or act on the addictive behavior.

> **If you fail to change the person you were when you came in, that person will take you out.** The person who comes into a meeting for the first time is a person who only knows how to live life while using or acting out. That person does not have life skills to deal with the normal occurrences that can happen in everyday life. The goal of the steps and recovery is to change, and if a person does not change, he or she will ultimately relapse.

> **Insanity is doing the same thing over and over again, expecting different results.** (paraphrased from Albert Einstein) This saying almost speaks for itself, but is particularly appropriate for the Second Step in recovery. If one expects to change, then he or she must take

different actions from those that resulted in the problem. By taking different actions, an individual in recovery will give him- or herself the opportunity to experience a difference result.

> **Isolation: It's the darkroom where I develop my negatives.** A quip that encapsulates what happens to someone who isolates and remains aloof from others in the twelve-step fellowship who could offer him or her help; only negativity can ensue. Recovery cannot occur when an individual is acting alone or refusing assistance from others in recovery. An isolated person tends to rely more and more heavily upon his or her character defects in order to cope with life. Dependence on defects is the "default position" of the person in order to fulfill his or her needs or wants; unfortunately, it often leads to relapse.

> **It Works! or It works if you work it!** A slogan affirming the idea that the twelve-step program is a success and people can and do recover— but only if they themselves work the program.

> **It's hard to be grateful when you're hateful, or It's hard to be hateful when you're grateful.** Gratitude does not come naturally to people in active addiction who always want "more, more, more." But developing gratitude is a necessary component of twelve-step recovery. Being aware of when one is feeling "hateful" and replacing that feeling with gratitude helps recovering individuals maintain contact with their higher power and with the fellowship.

> **It's okay to visit the past, just don't bring a suitcase.** During a Fourth Step inventory, a recovering person will need to review the past and write about his or her experiences, in order to take an honest self-assessment and make as thorough a house-cleaning as possible. But wallowing in guilt over past misdeeds is not helpful to the recovery process. The past is examined and past behaviors are noted in order that these behaviors may be avoided in future. Past wrongs are noted in order that amends may be made; however, the past is not a stick the recovering person uses to beat up him- or herself. Once the past is understood, it is put in its rightful place, and the individual moves on with recovery.

> **Juggling is not balancing.** It's an understatement to say that people in recovery have a tendency to bite off more than they can chew. They will take on multiple projects or responsibilities, have difficulty saying no, and will spread themselves too thin especially when new to recovery.

> **Just because you *have* a pain, doesn't mean you have to *be* one.** Walking through pain is challenging, even for a person with long-term recovery. The tendency is for a recovering person who is in pain to act out by lashing out at others. It is the goal of a recovering person to walk through emotional or physical pain by acknowledging feelings of discomfort, anger, sadness, etc. without lashing out at other people.

> **Just for today. (See also: One day at a time.)** A slogan in twelve-step programs used as a reminder for members that they only need to concentrate on not using or dealing with a situation right now, in the present. Newcomers, especially, can become discouraged at the thought of abstaining for the rest of their lives, but the thought of doing so "just for today" is less daunting and feels more attainable.

Additionally, people in recovery have a tendency to project thoughts into the future or to dwell on memories and patterns of the past and this deprives them of living in the moment, which is where recovery actually occurs. Worry and frustration about potential outcomes robs individuals of life in the moment, prevents them from embracing recovery, and can often lead to destructive behavior in an attempt to control an outcome.

Just for Today also is the name of the daily meditation book of Narcotics Anonymous.

> **Keep coming back.** The Third Tradition says the only requirement of a twelve-step program is the desire to stop using, drinking, or acting out on a particular manifestation of addiction. If an individual relapses, his or her "membership" is not "revoked." The important thing is for him or her to get back to a meeting and start over again.

› **Learn to listen and listen to learn.** The hardest thing for people to understand when they are new is that those who have been in recovery for a period of time can often empathize with many of the feelings the new person is going through. The new person needs to hear what it is like to stay clean or abstinent and work steps. The new person needs to listen to what he or she needs to do—the action he or she must take—in order to get another day clean/sober/abstinent. Recovery groups are not about sharing all of one's feelings so much as they are about getting support in the action and steps that must be taken in order to stay in recovery.

› **Let go and let God.** A phrase that comes out of the Third Step, which calls for turning one's will over to that of a power greater than oneself. Many people in the program use the word God as a sort of shorthand for higher power, but they do not necessarily mean a traditional, religious concept of God. This slogan is merely advising the individual to stop worrying about matters he or she cannot control and accept that these things can and will work out, according to the will of God or a higher power.

› **Letting go of the baggage.** In order to move forward in recovery, the recovering person must let go of those aspects from the past that do not serve him or her. These are often called resentments and must be dealt with. This happens formally with a sponsor in the Fourth and Fifth Steps. As people progress in recovery, "baggage" is picked up again, and they usually need to let go of this baggage regularly. The Tenth Step is very helpful with this process of letting go on a regular basis.

› **Life is painful. Misery is optional.** While it is virtually impossible to avoid pain—be it caused by the loss of a loved one, a relationship, financial security, or a job—the extent to which a person dwells on that pain is entirely up to him or her. Some of life's events are painful; it's the emotional response that generates *misery*. Through regular step work, meeting attendance, and contact with a support group, a person can avoid being miserable, although no one has ever been able to avoid pain.

> **Live in the solution.** The solution this phrase refers to is the Twelve Steps. Working and applying the Twelve Steps is a process that one must continue on a regular basis in order to face and solve life's problems. The steps are not an aspirin or a band-aid to be resorted to after the fact; they should be worked consistently and applied to the best of one's ability if a person's life is to improve.

> **Living life on life's terms.** The object of twelve-step programs is to live in recovery and stay clean/sober/abstinent; this means not relapsing no matter what life throws at one. This may mean staying clean and abstinent through the death of a loved one, divorce, the loss of jobs, or sometimes just simply a bad day or a string of bad days. It is not always the tragedies in life that can cause a relapse. Sometimes it is just going through life and becoming complacent about one's recovery, drifting away from meetings and others in recovery, and forgetting about the "basics of the program," which can and often does lead to a relapse.

> **Living the program.** To live the program means bringing what you learn in the program into every area of your life. (See also "walking the talk.") This saying ties back to several of the steps, including Steps Ten and Twelve, taking a regular personal inventory and practicing principles in all of one's affairs helps one live in the program.

> **Meeting makers make it.** Those who attend meetings regularly, in whatever twelve-step fellowship they belong to, tend to have a higher success rate at staying clean or abstinent. Meetings help form the basis of working a program.

> **Milestones of recovery (birthdays and anniversaries).** Typically, milestones of recovery in twelve-step programs are at thirty, sixty, and ninety days; six and nine months (and in some fellowships, eighteen months); and every 365 days clean (annually) or abstinent thereafter. Milestones are usually acknowledged at a meeting, either weekly or monthly, in a variety of different ways, according to local and fellowship custom.

> **No is a complete sentence.** One of the most difficult things for many people in recovery is to set and maintain boundaries. Early in recovery an individual may feel that he or she needs to explain why he or she cannot spend time with someone who is still in active addiction. Simply saying "no" without an explanation is completely healthy, acceptable, and sufficient.

> **No major decisions in your first year.** A person entering recovery is on the brink of a new way of life. Removing drugs, alcohol, and addictive behaviors, while healthy and necessary, requires a great deal of adjustment and commitment. Without active addiction, the recovering person is now swamped with new sensations—feelings and emotions masked by active addiction must now be processed in a natural and healthy way. Additional stresses, like changing jobs, relationship partners, or homes can often be too overwhelming during the first year. Newcomers to recovery usually feel a surge of energy and purposefulness, but it's best to use those impulses to concentrate on building the foundation that can support their new lives in recovery.

Embarking on new relationships, careers, etc. may provide a euphoric distraction from the difficult work of staying clean/sober/abstinent and may derail an individual's recovery.

> **No matter what your past, you have a spotless future.** The past is the past, and cannot be changed, but the future lies ahead, unblemished. Following a program of recovery can help it stay that way.

> **One day at a time (See also: Just for today).** This slogan expresses the truth underpinning all twelve-step programs; that all we can do is stay clean/sober/abstinent in the present moment. The old timer with twenty-four years is no more clean/sober/abstinent than the newcomer with twenty-four hours; each one is in recovery today; each could relapse tomorrow. This is the basis of much of the philosophy of acceptance, humility, honesty, tolerance, and willingness that is found in twelve-step recovery.

› **People who don't go to meetings don't hear about what happens to people who don't go to meetings.** In meetings, it's not uncommon to hear from a new person who is coming back from a relapse. More often than not that person will share about what happened before the relapse, i.e., he or she was not going to meetings and/or not calling his or her sponsor. People who are not at the meeting never get the chance or opportunity to hear from the people who are suffering as a result of not doing the simple, basic, and fundamental things that help one stay clean, sober, or abstinent.

› **Plan plans, not results.** Regardless of the "one day at a time" or "just for today" philosophy that is key to staying clean or abstaining, over time, a recovering person will likely become successful at making and keeping plans. This is fine as long as he or she realizes that plans have a way of working out differently than he or she wishes.

› **Principles before personalities.** From the Twelfth Tradition, the idea is to practice the spiritual principles learned through working the Twelve Steps regardless of the people involved. The practice of putting principles ahead of any personal differences ensures that regardless of the people (personalities) involved in any situation, the recovering person practices the concepts learned through working the steps.

› **Procrastination is fear in five syllables.** People in recovery sometimes put off doing something (like making amends) because of fear—fear of losing control of the outcome, fear of failure, or even fear of success.

› **Projection—living in the wreckage of the future.** Most people can become overwhelmed by thinking about the future, particularly in early recovery. One must live in the present day, based on what is happening during that day, and leave the results to a higher power or the process of recovery, while doing the daily footwork to stay clean or maintain abstinence regardless of what happens in the future, without reservations.

› **Recovery is a journey, not a destination (See also: Easy does it, and Recovery is a process, not an event).** Most individuals in active addiction are almost always more interested in instant gratification. The disease of addiction is the disease of "more is not enough" and "instant gratification takes too long." Impatience bedevils these people, and the time required to work on recovery can seem impossibly long for those who are used to changing their feelings in the time it takes to swallow a pill or a drink. It is important to remember that the Twelve Steps will change one's life, but will do so slowly.

› **Recovery is an action word.** This is said to imply that recovery means actually doing things such as getting and using a sponsor to work the Twelve Steps, attending meetings, reaching out to others in recovery, and sponsoring other members of the program an individual attends. Recovery is not simply a thing or state of mind that an individual is in, but instead, is something that a person must practice regularly in order to maintain freedom from active addiction.

› **Regardless of…** Just as addiction can happen to anyone, recovery can happen for anyone—believer or nonbeliever, old or young, gay or straight, married or single, educated or uneducated, jobless or employed, rich or poor, black, white, red, yellow, or any combination thereof. And a person in recovery can remain in recovery, regardless of any circumstance or misfortune.

› **Show up to grow up.** The most important part of recovery is the act of "showing up" —to meetings, service commitments, commitments with one's friends, employer, or sponsor, and "showing up" for oneself through doing step work.

› **Stick with the winners.** Who are the winners? The ones who are successful in recovery. This doesn't mean materially, but spiritually. Winners are the ones who are living a good and worthwhile life in recovery. These are usually the people who show up for meetings, who work steps, who are of service in the program, and who are good examples of how recovery works in a person's life.

> **Surrender to win.** Surrender is a key principle of the First Step. Part one of the step is acceptance of the disease of addiction or surrendering to the idea that one is powerless over the disease of addiction. Part two of that step is continual surrender by not using or acting on a behavior, and instead, focusing on taking action in recovery.

> **Take the program seriously, not yourself.** A benefit of recovery is the ability to laugh at oneself or difficult situations because the recovering person knows that he is she is not in control—only responsible for "the footwork."

> **Take what you need, leave the rest.** Much of the language and philosophy of twelve-step recovery is strange and perplexing to the newcomer. The advice to "take what you need and leave the rest," among other things, means to embrace what makes sense to you in early recovery, and set the rest aside. You may come back to it with greater understanding when you have more time in recovery.

Additionally, a newcomer to meetings may notice that because of the freedom to share "from the heart," some things are shared that are perplexing, odd, or downright obnoxious. Some people do take advantage of this opportunity to have the undivided attention of the group, and instead of sharing about the recovery process, working the steps, or their experiences, they want to talk about their day or go into some detail about something that others really do not want to hear. They may be insulting or insensitive to others in the room. Others may feel the need or desire to share directly "at" another or give advice or feedback directly to another member and engage in "cross-talk," which is generally frowned upon. Disregard the odd or bizarre things you may occasionally hear, and carry home the words that make sense to you.

> **Take your own inventory.** From the Fourth Step, which calls for a "searching and fearless moral inventory" of one's self. One should look at his or her own behaviors, rather than judge others for theirs. Looking at the character defects of others will not help a person work on his or her character defects.

> **Taking responsibility for my own recovery.** Recovery is a personal process; no one else can "make" you recover. Friends and family would have done it by now if it were possible. A person in recovery must take responsibility for attending meetings, finding and working with a sponsor, meeting commitments, and working the steps.

> **Talking out of the side of your neck.** Futile or fruitless, worthless talk. May also mean lying or speaking about things that one does not fully understand or have sufficient information to speak about in order to appear knowledgeable or important.

> **Terminally unique/Terminal uniqueness.** A feeling that one is different from other, ordinary mortals is common among many individuals in recovery. This can be fatal if it prevents a person from seeing that he or she is no different from others in recovery and constitutes a reservation in a member's program. All twelve-step programs are founded on the assumption that it is the common bond of addiction, shared among all members, that is the key to recovery. The healing that takes place when one person in recovery helps another is believed to be more effective in treating addiction than any other single thing (e.g., therapy, religion, etc.).

> **The elevator is broken. Use the steps.** There is no easy way to the recovery process. The process is simple, but it requires work. Those who suffer from addiction are usually looking for instant gratification or an "elevator," rather than doing the work necessary in the "steps," otherwise known as the Twelve Steps.

> **The nature of recovery.** The nature of recovery is the process of working the steps and practicing spiritual principles such as compassion, tolerance, acceptance, honesty, open-mindedness, and willingness.

> **The next indicated step (or taking the next right step).** Rather than focusing on the rest of one's life or major choices, a recovering person may be better served by just focusing on what he or she needs to do next.

› **The outsides don't match the insides.** The "outside" of someone's life could look really good, but he or she may be falling apart on the inside because of not taking care of the things he or she needs to be taking care of, such as working steps, attending meetings, doing service work, etc. Likewise, things may appear to be falling apart on the outside for a person, but if his or her program is intact and robust, then that is what is important. If a person is diligently working on his or her recovery it will often feel uncomfortable, but from the outside people will see that person as doing really well because their actions are that of someone embracing recovery.

› **The road gets narrower.** The idea of the "road getting narrower" is a popular one in many twelve-step programs, referring to the metaphorical road that one travels along in recovery. It is said to mean that as one continues on the path of recovery, old behaviors that were once acceptable may need to be discarded. Lying, cheating, stealing, cruelty, intolerance, etc. are no longer options; as the "road" narrows, these practices no longer fit. As a person becomes more focused on his or her recovery, the ways that person can "act out" are far more limited. Without over-interpreting this saying, some believe that the road getting narrower implies that one has fewer ways of acting on addiction the longer he or she stays in recovery, but that one's opportunities for growth and life actually grow wider.

› **The rooms/these rooms.** The meeting rooms where twelve-step program meetings are held.

› **The steps are the answer/The answer is in the steps.** When a member is confused about a right course of action, rather than listen to another member who may be more than willing to dole out advice, the member would be better served by remembering that the program is based on the Twelve Steps, and within the steps is a right and safe approach to any question or problem. Working the steps with a sponsor will help members deal with "life on life's terms." Every problem life presents has been dealt with in most twelve-step programs, and though the programs are not designed to answer all of life's questions, they provide a framework that allows the individual members to accept "life on life's terms" and remain in recovery.

> **The steps keep us from suicide; the traditions, from homicide.** The steps are considered a personal process, helping a person in recovery to build and heal his or her relationship with him- or herself. The traditions, while written in relation to the group or fellowship, have often been studied by individuals who view them as guidelines for dealing with other people in the program's service structure.

> **The three most dangerous words for a person in recovery: "I've been thinking."** Recognizes that the thinking of an individual in recovery has not, in many instances in the past, resulted in safe or sane decision-making. A lighthearted reminder to the newcomer to discuss any new ideas or projects with a sponsor or friends with more time in recovery, at least until he or she has had the opportunity to work through the Twelve Steps. After a person has been in recovery for a period of time and worked the steps, he or she can begin to trust his or her thinking to a larger degree.

> **The war is over and you lost.** A friendly reminder that one's addiction is always going to be stronger than oneself, and that the only way to "win" is to surrender. Sometimes said to a newcomer who may be trying to justify his or her continued using or acting on addictive behavior and to prompt the person to accept that he or she can no longer continue to use or act out.

> **Today is a gift; that's why it's called the present.** Every day that someone with addiction abstains is a successful day.

› **Trying is dying.** This saying came from the idea that many people in recovery will use the word "try" as an excuse for not actually doing something. They may say they will try to work the steps, try to call their sponsor, or try to remain abstinent, and the response from another recovering member may be "trying is dying," because someone in recovery simply needs to commit to doing that thing he or she is actually resisting doing. To say that one is "trying" is often a cop-out, excuse, or reservation in one's program.

› **Turn it over.** In the Third Step the recovering person is asked to turn his or her will over to a power greater than him- or herself. The process of "turning it over" means to practice program principles instead of acting out in destructive behaviors; it can also be accomplished through prayer and meditation. The act of surrendering a situation, person, etc. to the care of a loving higher power.

› **Walking the talk/Walk the walk, don't just talk the talk/Watch your feet.** What people say in meetings is meaningless unless their "talk" is matched with their "walk;" that is, they practice the principles of the program outside the meeting, with others in and out of the program, to the best of their ability on a daily basis.

› **We grow up in public.** The process of recovery is a "public" process in that one must reveal him- or herself in meetings with other recovering people and with a sponsor. It also is a process that teaches to many the things they should have learned as they were growing up had they not begun to live in their disease. These things include how to be a friend, a parent, an employee, etc. As people learn and grow in the group, many feel they are "growing up" in public.

> **When the pain of staying the same is greater than the fear of change, we'll change.** People with the disease of addiction will become accustomed to the pain they experience from doing the same thing over and over again, even knowing what the results will be. They are familiar with that pain and know how to deal with it. This often stands in the way of surrendering and stopping that particular action and starting another; the fear of the unknown is greater than the pain of the familiar; however, once the pain of the familiar becomes great enough, a person will stop and face the fear of what the new action may offer.

> **Where-and-when.** A term used for a schedule of recovery meetings in a particular area, also known as a meeting list. The meeting lists for local meetings, which are usually updated regularly, contain information such as meeting location, address, meeting time, meeting classification (whether the meeting is open, closed, a literature study, speaker meeting, etc.), whether the meeting is smoking/non-smoking, or handicapped-accessible. Planning which meetings to attend is helpful to the newly recovering person.

> **Would you rather be right or happy?** The most difficult thing for someone in recovery is admitting that he or she was/is wrong. To admit when one is wrong frees one from having to cling to a posture of righteousness and enables one to embrace a different path. This is also a reference to being open-minded, a key principle to working the Second Step.

> **Yesterday is history, tomorrow a mystery.** The only thing a recovering person can do about the past is work a program of recovery today. Even making amends requires working a program in the here-and-now. One does not know what will happen in the future, so all a recovering person can do is focus on what he or she can do for his or her recovery each day.

› **Yets.** Things a person has not done up to a given point in time. The idea that although a particular situation or event (e.g., divorce, a prison term, loss of children, etc.) has not occurred in someone's life due to his or her addiction, it is likely to happen in the future should they relapse.

In sharing at a meeting, people may say of something, "That is one of my 'yets.'" Admitting one has "yets" is admitting that while one has not plumbed the absolute depths of degradation, it could happen yet, if one were to relapse. Could contribute to reservations, e.g., "I never prostituted myself for drugs; maybe I'm not a real addict," or "I never got a DUI; maybe I'm not a real alcoholic." These things are examples of "yets"; things that have not yet happened, but that most likely will if a person in recovery relapses.

› **You are a member when you say you are.** There is no application process nor are there dues or fees for twelve-step program membership. The only requirement is a desire to stop using/drinking/over-eating/gambling/etc.

› **You cannot be in fear and faith at the same time.** Living in faith means trusting that all will be well; living in fear means dreading that all will be ill. All human beings, not just those in recovery, experience fear; it's a natural and sometimes useful part of life that helps one avoid dangers. But for people with the disease of addiction, living in fear is part of what led to their addictive behavior; trying to evade those fears led them to the escapism of using/drinking/acting out/etc.

The attributes of fear and faith are at odds; one cannot act on fear-based addictive thinking or take character-defect-based actions and at the same time act in faith, recovery-oriented, spiritual-principle-based actions. It is virtually impossible for one to practice a spiritual principle and its defect-based opposite at the same time. This slogan is often misinterpreted or misrepresented to make one believe that he or she cannot feel fear or faith at the same time. However, one of the first things a newcomer learns in recovery is that feelings are often not based in reality; that just because a person feels, desires, or has a thought to perform a certain action, he or she is not bound to perform that action, e.g., one can be afraid of using drugs—a healthy fear—but one does not need to use nor does that mean that person's recovery is in danger.

› **You can't get indigestion from swallowing your pride.** It is often humbling to admit that one has been acting out in his or her disease, that he or she is powerless, or that his or her behavior has been based in his or her disease. But admitting these things, or "swallowing one's pride," is necessary if one is to become open-minded to taking different actions. If one is to do a thorough Eighth or Ninth Step, it will be necessary to set aside pride and admit prior wrongs in order to get the relief promised by the program.

› **You can't save your face and your ass at the same time.** Recovering people who try to maintain the appearance or illusion of having a manageable life run the risk of relapse. A person in recovery must accept and admit powerlessness and unmanageability in those areas he or she wishes to change in order to recover. It is also necessary, when a person in recovery is in pain or needs help, to reach out to others and admit that he or she is in pain.

Some Character Defects and Manifestations

We can define character as a person's moral makeup, observable through his or her habits, personality traits, and general disposition—these include such qualities as kindness, generosity, humility, and honesty, which are character assets. Character defects are the negative qualities that also constitute a person's moral makeup, such as pride, fear, laziness, greed, egotism, lust, and so forth. These traits exist alongside each other, but it is the defects that are addressed by the Twelve Steps.

For a newcomer to twelve-step recovery, the idea of assessing his or her own character defects may be off-putting or worse, irrelevant or "quaint." It is not uncommon for many people in recovery to be wracked with guilt at all the wreckage they have left behind in the course of their active disease. Working Step Six may appear to be overwhelming when people look at the specific character defects that need to be addressed in order to change. But in order to live a life of recovery that will allow individuals to right those guilt-inducing wrongs, a Sixth Step must be worked.

Even those who are willing to "give it a go," and make an attempt to work the steps may have no idea what sorts of attributes constitute defects of character. The following pages list some of the commonly encountered character defects that arise in working a twelve-step recovery program. Please note that these definitions are not complete—they relate to the words only as they relate to the idea of character as used in twelve-step recovery. The list is, of necessity, incomplete; you will surely think of other possible entries as you work the steps yourself.

Note: *Although the defects themselves may be summarized by umbrella terms like "pride" or "greed," the following list includes the behaviors, or manifestations, of the defects, which are easier to identify. So you will find "arrogance" and "competitiveness" listed along with the overarching terms like pride or greed.*

ABUSIVENESS

Viciousness, rudeness, cruelty. To cause physical, emotional, or spiritual injury to another.

AGGRESSION

Force, insistence, belligerence. (At odds with calm, serenity.) Cause of behaving in a hostile, overly intense, or harsh manner. (Note: One can be assertive without being aggressive.)

ALIENATION/ALIENATING

Estrangement, distancing, hostility. Withdrawing from others or being unresponsive to them; isolation or emotional detachment from others.

ARROGANCE

Haughtiness, overconfidence, superiority. Making claims to unwarranted importance or expecting special consideration out of overbearing pride.

BETRAYING

Revealing, divulging; violating someone else's trust or confidence. Being false or disloyal to. Breaking faith with another.

COMPETITIVENESS

Vying with others for domination, lacking a spirit of cooperation; cutthroat. Desiring one's own victory above all else.

COMPLAINING

Whiny, belligerent, irritable. Expressing feelings of pain, discomfort, or resentment.

COMPULSIVE

Obsessive, neurotic, uncontrollable. Caused or conditioned by obsession or fixation. A person with behavior patterns governed by a fixation.

CONDITIONAL

Restrictive, provisional, qualified. Dependent on certain situations or circumstances.

CRITICAL

Judgmental, unsympathetic, fault-finding. Judging self or others severely, reproaching, blaming, or disparaging.

DEFENSIVE

Self-protective, suspicious, distrustful. Constantly protecting oneself from criticism, exposure of one's shortcomings, or other real or perceived threats to the ego. Intended to withstand or deter aggression or attack.

DEMANDING

Challenging, needy, dissatisfied. Requiring much effort or attention. To ask for urgently or peremptorily. Claiming as one's due.

DESTRUCTIVE

Damaging, detrimental, injurious. Causing or creating ruin. Designed or tending to disprove or discredit.

DISCONNECT(ED)

To sever or interrupt the link or relationship between self and others or a higher power.

DISHONORABLE (NESS)

Lacking integrity, unprincipled, shameful. Behavior that is unethical.

DISSATISFIED

Malcontent, disgruntled, unhappy. Chronically discontented. Having expectations that never seem to be met, chronically displeased or frustrated.

DOUBT

Uncertainty, reservation, misgiving.

DRAMATIC

Inauthentic, staged or stagy, exaggerated. Overly expressive or emotional; theatrical.

EGOTISM

Selfishness, self-centeredness, insensitivity. Lack of consideration of others.

ENVY

Covetousness, desire, resentful. A feeling of discontent and resentment aroused by the desire for the possessions or qualities of another.

ESCAPISM

Distraction, avoidance, diversion. The tendency to get away from reality or routine by indulging in daydreaming, fantasizing, or entertainment.

EXTREMISM

Radicalism, fanaticism, fervor. Advocating or resorting to measures beyond the norm. Making situations or conditions appear much more or much less than what they are.

FANTASTIC(AL) THINKING

To engage in unrealistic, imaginary, or wholly fictitious thinking about the nature of the world and one's place in it; to refuse to accept reality in favor of imaginative scenarios.

GLUTTONY

Greed, excessive or extreme. Relates to an excess in eating or drinking.

GRANDIOSITY

Pretentiousness, lavishness, ostentation. Characterized by greatness of scope or intent; or by feigned or affected grandeur.

GRANDSTANDING

Show off, showboat, ham it up. To perform ostentatiously so as to impress an audience.

GREED

Insatiable, self-indulgent, gluttony. An excessive desire to acquire or possess more than what one needs or deserves, especially with respect to material wealth.

HATRED

Loathing, revulsion, detestation. Demonstration of disgust or extreme animosity or hostility.

INCONSIDERATE

Thoughtless, uncharitable, insensitive to the feelings of others. Displaying a lack of care or concern, especially toward others.

INCONSISTENCY

Irregularity, contradiction, incompatible. Displaying or marked by a lack of regularity, erratic. Lacking in correct logical relation; not in agreement or harmony.

INSECURITY

Timidness, uncertain, lack of confidence. Feeling doubtful, inadequate, or unprotected. Lacking emotional stability or self-confidence; plagued by anxiety.

INSENSITIVE

Unfeeling, unsympathetic, tactless. Not physically or emotionally sensitive to the needs of others. Emotionally or physically numb. Lacking in sensitivity to the feelings or circumstances of others.

IRRESPONSIBLE

Negligent, reckless, careless. Displaying lack of responsibility or sense of responsibility; unreliable or untrustworthy. Not mentally or financially fit to assume responsibility.

JEALOUSY

Envy, covetousness, possessiveness. Over-concern for the actions of others and feeling threatened that such actions may deprive one of a need or want. Resentful desire for another's advantages. Unreasonable belief that one's own relationships, possessions, or attributes may be lost or taken by another.

JUSTIFICATION

Validation, rationalization, excuse. Something, such as a fact or circumstance, that explains sufficiently for/of the purpose.

LAZINESS

Lethargy, idleness, sloth. Resistant to work or exertion; idle, slow-moving.

LOW TOLERANCE FOR FRUSTRATION

Causing one to give up before accomplishing a purpose or fulfilling a desire when thwarted. Causing feelings of discouragement or bafflement.

LUST

Intense sexual hunger, longing or desire; usually termed lust when unaccompanied by love.

MANIPULATION

Exploitation, handling, coercing. The act or practice of influencing others' behavior by intimidating, bullying, lying, or pressuring them. The state of being manipulated. Shrewd or devious management usually for one's own advantage. Not necessarily violent or overt.

MATERIALISM

Avariciousness, greediness, covetousness. A great or excessive regard for worldly concerns. The idea that physical well-being and worldly possessions constitute the greatest good and highest value in life, usually at the expense of the spiritual.

MEAN

Unkind, cruel, malicious. The state of being selfish, stingy, hostile, or aggressive to another. Spiteful or callous. Unusually or excessively marked by animosity.

MORBID

Gloomy, melancholic, dark. Psychologically unhealthy or unwholesome. Characterized by preoccupation with unwholesome thoughts or feelings.

NEEDY

Deprived, needing affection, impoverished. Emotional state of exhibiting an intense need for love or other emotional support.

NEGATIVE

Pessimistic, unenthusiastic, downbeat. Indicating opposition or resistance. Having no positive features. Exhibiting features that are not positive or constructive.

NOSINESS

Over-inquisitiveness, snooping, prying. Given to excessive prying into the affairs of others.

NOT-SUPPORTIVE/UNSUPPORTIVE

Unaccommodating, disobliged, selfish. Not furnishing support or assistance.

OBSESSIVE

Compulsive, fanatical, fixated. Relating to, characteristic of, or causing an obsession; the uncontrollable desire to perform an irrational act. Excessive in degree or nature.

OVERLY ANALYTICAL

Excessively critical, methodical, obsessive. An obsession with breaking down all the parts of a thought, feeling, situation, or scenario and thereby complicating things that may have been otherwise simple.

PASSIVE

Submissive, unreceptive, inert, Receiving or subjected to an action without responding or initiating an action in return. Accepting or submitting to a situation or action of another without objection, resistance, or verbal complaint.

PEOPLE-PLEASING

Codependent, lack of self-esteem, negative disregard of self. Providing a function in order to make another satisfied, often at the expense of the person performing said action.

PREJUDICE

Bias, narrow-mindedness, bigotry. An adverse judgment or opinion formed beforehand or without knowledge or examination of the facts. A preconceived preference or idea. Irrational suspicion or hatred of a particular group, race, or religion.

PRIDE

Smugness, vanity, conceit. Considered a character defect when it becomes arrogant or disdainful conduct or treatment; haughtiness. Healthy pride is a sense of one's own proper dignity or value; self-respect. Pleasure or satisfaction taken in an achievement, a possession, or an association.

PROCRASTINATION

Postpone, put off, dawdling. To delay needlessly or put off doing something, especially out of habitual laziness.

REJECT

Decline, rebuff, deny. To refuse to accept, submit to, believe, or make use of. To refuse to recognize or give consideration to a person. To discard as defective or useless; throw away.

RESENTFUL

Bitter, indignant, angry. To feel indignant; ill will. Carrying forth past trauma, pain, or harm into a present situation and often affecting present decisions. An unaddressed grudge or animosity that usually becomes compounded.

RIGID

Inflexible, unbending, stiff. Fixed in idea, attitude, perception, or action.

RUMINATE/RUMINATION

Reflect, ponder, think over. Constant dwelling on one's own thoughts.

SABOTAGE/SABOTAGING

Damage, disruption, interference. Destruction of property or obstruction of normal operations. Treacherous action to defeat or hinder a current path, cause, or an endeavor. The deliberate or unconscious destruction or derailment of one's life.

SARCASM/SARCASTIC

Irony, mockery, scorn. Using words as a weapon against another person, often disguised as humor, but at the expense of another. Passive-aggressive behavior toward another. Making false or inaccurate statements with the appearance of humor or wit.

SELF-CENTERED

Self-absorbed, egotistical, self-seeking. Engrossed in oneself and one's own affairs; selfish.

SELF-HATRED (SELF-ABASEMENT)

Self-loathing, disgust of oneself, extreme dislike of oneself. Intense hostility, degradation, or humiliation of oneself, especially because of feelings of guilt or inferiority.

SELF-IMPORTANCE

Conceit, egocentric, narcissistic. Excessively high regard for one's own importance or station. Thinking too highly of oneself; arrogant, boastful, vain.

SELFISH

Greedy, self-centered, egocentric. Concerned chiefly or only with oneself. Arising from, characterized by, or showing selfishness.

SLY

Cunning, crafty, devious. Adept in being cunning. Lacking candor. Can also mean playfully mischievous; roguish.

STANDOFFISH

Distant, disdainful, aloof, Marked by excessive pride in oneself and disdain for others; snobbish.

UNFORGIVING

Intolerant, merciless, vindictive. Reluctant or refusing to forgive. Providing little or no opportunity to forestall undesired results or mistakes.

UNWILLINGNESS

Refusal, disinclination, obstinate. Not willing; reluctance to perform an action.

VENGEFUL

Resentful, vindictive, ruthless. Desiring vengeance or being vindictive. Proceeding from a desire for revenge or serving to exact vengeance.

VIOLENT

Brutal, sadistic, vicious. Marked by, acting with, or resulting from great force. Having or showing great emotional force.

NOTES